Help Your Teenager Succeed at School

Other parenting books from Continuum

Getting Your Little Darlings to Behave – Sue Cowley

A Parent's Guide to Primary Schools – Katy Byrne and Harvey McGavin

Educating Your Child at Home – Jane Lowe and Alan Thomas

Help Your Teenager Succeed at School

A Parent's Guide

Michael Papworth

continuum
LONDON • NEW YORK

Continuum
The Tower Building
11 York Road
London
SE1 7NX

15 East 26th Street
New York, NY 10010

British Library Cataloguing-in-Publication Data
A catalogue record for this book is available from the British Library.

ISBN: 0 8264 7424 1 (paperback)

Library of Congress Cataloguing-in-Publication Data
A catalogue record for this book is available from the Library of Congress.

Typeset by Fakenham Photosetting Limited, Fakenham, Norfolk.
Printed and bound in Great Britain by Hobbs the Printers, Hampshire.

Contents

Acknowledgements

My first and extra-special thanks go to my children, Fred, Joe and Sarah and their delightful mother, my wife, Jennie. They know by experience that this book was written from the heart. Their help and constant support and understanding during the research, preparation and writing was vital, and without it I couldn't have written it.

I have had a great deal of help from a whole host of wonderful people. Some of them are parents, teachers, or professionals in the field of childcare, and I wish to thank all of them. They have given freely of their time, knowledge and special wisdoms. In particular, I wish to thank three wonderful headteachers for their time and advice. They are Clive Corbett of Pershore High School, Bernard Roberts of Prince Henry's High School, Evesham and Clive Owen of Frankley Community High School, Birmingham.

Special thanks are due to Alexandra at Continuum for continued understanding, suggestions, support and advice.

However, my greatest and most heartfelt thanks go to my mum. She raised my sister and me almost single-handedly, as my dad was a sailor and nearly always at sea. Her positive parenting and practical demonstrations of love and support have guided us both through life. Thanks, Mum. Hey, look at me. I'm an author now!

Introduction

Michelangelo Buonarroti was probably the most brilliant sculptor who ever lived. There is a story that, one day, a small boy sat watching as he was chipping away at a rough lump of marble. 'What are you doing?' asked the child. 'There's an angel trapped inside the marble,' replied Michelangelo, 'and I'm releasing it.' It appears as if we parents are trying to do something similar. Inside the rough lumps that our teenage children often seem to be, there's an adult waiting to emerge. The stone that Michelangelo had to work on was very hard and Michelangelo worked with basic tools. Our teenagers can be hard at times and we only have basic tools.

But there the analogy ends. Michelangelo used a hammer and chisels to knock lumps off hunks of lifeless stone. Teenagers are not stone. They have deep and delicate feelings that are undergoing rapid changes due to their biology and their changing position in the world. No-one is going to release an angel by knocking lumps off a teenager. That's a recipe for creating a devil.

Some time ago, I heard a story about a man who was playing soccer with his young children in the back garden. Mum shouted from the kitchen window, 'Hey, mind you don't scuff up the grass.' Dad shouted back, 'We aren't raising grass, love. We're raising kids.' It seems to me that he had the right idea.

There are three basic ideas running through this book. The first idea is that love conquers all. We are parents. We can't help but feel a deep love and affection for our children. Even at the times they appear to be unlovable and difficult, we love them still. The tragedy is that we don't always show it. And there's the rub. It's not enough just to love our teenagers: we also need to let them know they are loved. And even more than loved, they need to feel respected and valued. It isn't always easy, but no-one ever said it was going to be. The book contains plenty of advice, and simple and practical ideas showing the things you can do to make it a little bit easier.

The second idea is that you don't make people do good by making them feel bad about themselves. It is vital that your teenager sees the world as a positive place and sees the positive contribution that he or she has to make to it. Teenagers are idealistic and see the world in black and white. This often causes them to get depressed and rebellious. Your contribution is to blend with your teenager and try to see the world through his or her eyes. Then, once you have empathy and understanding, you can guide your teenager towards a good reality.

The third idea is that the only way to get people to do what you want them to do is to help them want to do it. It often seems as if raising a teenager is a constant battle. It's not exactly an epic battle of good against evil, but the basic ideas aren't too far away from each other. When you take the time to stand back and look at life, you'll find that there is much more space for agreement than for conflict – you both want a lot of the same things. The secret is to avoid the conflict and reach agreements agreeably.

The book refers to Mum and Dad, but doesn't presuppose marriage or even a couple raising the children. Everything is equally applicable to single-parent families.

Read the book and you'll be a better-informed and happier parent. Do the action exercises at the end of most of the chapters and you'll raise a happy, healthy teenager. Moreover, he or she will be a happy, healthy teenager who cannot help but grow into a happy, healthy adult and be your friend for life.

ONE

Teenagers' Physical and Emotional Development

Start with the end in mind

The changes that take place in adolescents' bodies throughout puberty are truly amazing. In just a few short years, they go from being small children into being young adults ready to take their place in the world. These changes take place so rapidly that they can frequently cause great upset to the adolescents themselves, as well as their poor unsuspecting parents.

Teenagers are frequently described as being a different species. They aren't. Teenagers are human beings who just happen to be going through a very rapid state of change. All change is difficult to handle no matter what it is. When the changes are happening as rapidly as they do during adolescence, the difficulties are magnified.

We need to use language carefully here; adolescence and puberty are not the same thing at all, although they start at more or less the same time. Adolescence is the stage between child-like and adult thinking. Puberty is the stage between a child's and an adult body. One of the greatest difficulties facing parents and teenagers is that the physical and intellectual changes don't keep pace with one another.

Teenagers look at their almost-adult body and assume that they must have the adult intellect to go with it. They are mistaken! Adults look at the adult bodies and wonder when the adult behaviour will appear. Don't worry too much. Your lovely children will eventually emerge into lovely young adults. It's just that they have to go through a rather ugly lava-like adolescent stage first.

Puberty follows a predictable set of stages, and even the age it starts at can be roughly predicted. It usually starts at about the same age as it started for the same gender parent. The ages mentioned in the following sections are averages for white Caucasoid children in western societies. Children of other ethnicities have different averages, but nearly all fall well within the bands of normal development. Do you remember being told not to compare your toddler to others of the same age as they all develop differently? Well, all adolescents also develop during puberty at different rates and there is unlikely to be anything abnormal about your teenager.

Adolescence is far less predictable than puberty. Thinking abilities are a much more complex matter and develop according to the emotional and intellectual environment. If this environment is positive and supportive, there will probably be few major hiccups. If it isn't, there will almost certainly be big problems.

Having an understanding of the changes that take place and what happens is very reassuring. It will help you realize that the hormone-driven beast in your house really is a normal creature.

How puberty starts

It all starts in the brain. A tiny part of your brain called the hypothalamus produces a hormone called GnRH, which then causes another part of your brain called the pituitary gland to produce two more hormones called FSH and LH. These hormones cause the gonads (testicles in a boy and ovaries in a girl) to release sex hormones. These are testosterone for a boy and oestrogen for a girl. These hormones, in turn, cause the hypothalamus to produce less GnRH. It's a carefully balanced system similar to a thermostat at its lowest setting. As the hormone temperature warms up, the thermostat shuts the boiler down. As the hormone temperature cools down, the boiler is switched on again.

But during puberty, the hypothalamus becomes less and less sensitive to sex hormones. It's just like the thermostat becoming less sensitive. There's still balance, but the quantities of sex hormones increase, decrease, and swing between extremes. That's when things start to happen.

How boys' bodies grow

The earliest sign of puberty in boys is an increase in size of the scrotum and testicles. This normally starts anywhere between the ages of ten and fourteen, with an average age of about eleven and a half. You will probably not notice this as boys usually start to want privacy at this stage in their lives.

About a year or so later they will start a sudden growth spurt and typically grow in height by four inches or so per year. This is quite unmistakable. Apart from anything else, they will suddenly start to need new clothes and shoes with depressing regularity.

As bones don't grow at equal rates, they may start to look a little clumsy and gangly at this stage and even trip over themselves at times. Hands and feet grow the fastest. Arms and legs grow a little less fast, but faster than the bones of the upper body. Even the bones in the face grow at differing rates and can cause noses to grow out of proportion or jaws to lengthen. Everything does settle down eventually as the growth spurt slows and things begin to balance better, but it can be a traumatic time for a young boy. He is expecting manhood to come dashing towards him and what he finds is that his appearance is changing and he starts to look quite odd to himself. No-one else really notices, but he's very self-conscious at this stage.

The start of the growth spurt is followed a few months later by a lengthening and thickening of the penis. And about six months after that pubic hair starts to grow followed a little later by underarm hair. The average age for this is about fourteen.

At about this time (or maybe several years earlier), your son will start a lifelong relationship with one or more of his hands and masturbate regularly. Masturbation is not known to have any ill effects and is a thoroughly enjoyable experience, so let him get on with it. Just don't let on that you know. Once the hormones are really flowing, his voice begins to break and becomes deeper and more mature. By this stage, puberty is more than halfway over.

As boys continue to mature sexually, they begin to develop additional body oils. These react with natural bacteria on the skin and cause body odour. No longer will your son smell delightful when you cuddle him. (By this stage, he probably won't want you to cuddle him anyway.) Rather, he'll smell sweaty unless he is careful about his personal hygiene and showers or bathes daily. A shower or bath every morning and clean clothes should keep him tolerable. Anything less doesn't bear thinking about. Please point out to your son that, no, deodorants are not an alternative to washing. And as we all know, he won't start smelling any better as he grows older.

The final stage of puberty is when the growth spurt slows down and almost stops. Shoulders suddenly broaden and the boy starts to take on a manly appearance. The young body can now start giving more energy to putting meat on the skeleton and begins to fill out with muscle. Facial hair starts to appear at about the same time. The average age for this is about fifteen, but it can occur anywhere from about fourteen to seventeen or even later. Boys continue to grow slowly in stature and rapidly in muscle bulk, some into their early twenties.

It's a wonderful process to watch. To see a young boy of thirteen or so nearly double his body weight (typically from forty to seventy kilograms) and change into a fine, muscular young man of eighteen is one of nature's greatest wonders.

External physical changes of boys during puberty

Testicles and scrotum grow larger → Pubic hair starts to appear → Penis increases in length and girth → First ejaculation → Growth spurt starts → Growth spurt slows → Muscle bulk added and shoulders broaden → Facial hair and underarm hair appears → Final pubic hair pattern

How girls' bodies grow

The early changes that girls undergo in puberty are much more evident than those of boys. This is because they are visual as the changes in body shape are obvious.

The first external sign of puberty in girls is breast-budding which starts at an average age of eleven, but can start anywhere from nine to thirteen. Budding starts as small lumps under the nipples (or quite possibly under one nipple only – unequal breast growth is common). Before long, there will be a need for a trainer bra. This is more for comfort than for support.

A girl's first bra is usually an exciting time in a young girl's life. However, if the girl is an early developer, it can be a source of embarrassment. The best course of action here is to be open and honest and help your daughter to celebrate her impending womanhood and, if it makes her more comfortable, get her loose clothing to try to cover up developing breasts.

Of course, mothers remember this time from their own puberty and can easily relate to their daughter's feelings. Whilst adulthood is an everyday thing to Mum, it comes as a bit of a surprise to Miss Junior. It is a rather more difficult time for fathers. It can, and frequently does, come as a tremendous shock to notice one day that your lovely playful little girl has suddenly become a small object of desire to boys. Dad, your daughter won't share your feelings on the matter, so don't make any inappropriate remarks.

The first bra is followed within six months by a soft and downy growth of pubic hair. The full adult pattern of thick, curly hair won't develop until puberty is almost completed.

Up to about ten or eleven years of age, boys and girls grow at roughly the same rate and their average heights are nearly identical. Girls start their growth spurt a year or two earlier than boys (at an average age of ten or so) and they quickly become taller than boys. The boys don't start to catch up again for a couple of years.

During the growth spurt girls grow upwards and outwards and develop a more curvaceous, feminine shape. Breasts continue to grow and girls deposit fat round the thighs, hips and bum, and lose it from the waist. The pelvis also starts to widen in preparation for womanhood. By this stage, girls are

5

becoming used to their new developing body shape, but are not always pleased with it. In fact, being displeased is much more common.

Girls need a lot of help with this one. Nearly all girls are concerned that they are too fat or thin, too tall or short, top heavy or bottom heavy, and so forth. The strong probability is that your daughter is just right. There is no such thing as a universally perfect body shape – particularly during puberty when development is unequal. If your daughter eats the recommended quantities of healthy foods, gets lots of fresh air, exercise and rest, and grooms herself well, she will be close to perfect.

The next stage is the growth of underarm hair and this is followed within a few months by the first menstrual period. This should never come as a surprise to a girl. As long as she is aware of her course of development (and that is the purpose of this chapter), she should be well prepared for the things that are happening to her body. When periods start they are generally very irregular and only fall into the normal monthly cycle a year or more after the first period. Girls need to know that they can be fertile from the moment of their first period. There is always going to be the debate about internal or external sanitary protection, and this needs to be discussed with your daughter before her first period.

In the later stages of puberty, the feminine shape continues to develop and towards the end nipples become distinct from the surrounding areola. Most girls have almost reached their full adult height by age fifteen. Girls continue to develop a more feminine shape up to about eighteen or so.

External physical changes of girls during puberty

Breast buds appear → Pubic hair starts to appear → Growth spurt starts → Underarm hair starts to appear → Peak of growth spurt → First period → Final pubic hair pattern → Full breast growth

It ain't that simple

The previous two sections are only true for the vast majority of adolescents. There are always going to be factors which can cause differences. It is well known that deficient nutrition and inadequate rest can reduce physical growth and intellectual development. Inherited factors are also important. There are also likely to be other factors which can have effects. If things don't seem to be going according to plan, a visit to a doctor is advisable. When making the appointment you might ask to see the practice's paediatrics specialist. If the doctor suspects that anything is amiss, a blood sample may be taken for analysis.

A bit more about hormones

When teenagers are described as being hormone-driven, that's exactly what they are. Their brains and bodies are flooded with sex and growth hormones that are there and doing their job and much more besides.

Just imagine what would happen to your Great Uncle Bill's 1956 Hillman Minx if you filled it with nitro-charged dragster fuel and let it loose around a racetrack. Now imagine what happens when you fill a young teenage body and immature brain with hormone-charged blood and let it loose on an unsuspecting world. Yes, that's right! It's disaster in both cases. The Hillman's engine is going to get strained and its brakes aren't going to work too well. It's the same with teenagers. They are an accident looking for somewhere to happen.

Every woman knows what happens when hormone levels get disturbed. Even if she doesn't suffer with her periods herself, she will know many women who do. Every man knows someone about whom it is said, 'His bollocks rule his brain.' Hormones do what hormones do. They are the chemicals which control the working of your body and your brain. When the levels get upset, everything gets upset. And it is precisely for that reason that teenagers do what teenagers do. It's nothing personal against you, and most of them are not going to turn into sociopaths. It's neither more nor less than their wonderful, highly tuned bodies and brains going through an essential phase of life with variable quality fuel.

Emotions

I was lucky enough to be brought up in a pleasant village in industrial Lancashire, as it was then. During the summers, a travelling fair came to the village. From about age eight, I went there every evening with my mates. One summer, when I was thirteen, I went with my family to visit an old sea-faring friend of my father's down in London. There was a fair in the park. I suggested that I could go by myself. I was told that I couldn't – I would almost certainly be set upon and robbed. 'I can look after myself,' I said. 'Don't be so bloody stupid,' my father replied. I remember it well. It stung and hurt me very much.

When a similar situation arose with my own son, I forgot that time completely. I must have hurt him just as much as I was hurt myself. I'm not the only parent to make that kind of mistake. We adults always forget what it was like to be adolescents ourselves – and it doesn't help us.

Adolescence is a time of great emotional turmoil caused by more than just the hormones. It's also caused by a great (and frequently justified) sense that the adult world just doesn't understand and seems hell-bent on frustrating everything that adolescents want to do. We know that youngsters often need to be protected from themselves, but they just don't see it. Is it any wonder that adolescents can get angry and react badly?

If there is any wonder about it at all, it is that the vast majority of adolescents grow into being such decent people as they do. When you consider the problems that they face and the unfeeling reactions of most adults, some schools, the police, the Government and the media it will probably cause you wonder as well.

Before we mention the problems that adolescence can bring, I have to say that many youngsters go through this essential stage of life with few problems. Nearly everyone can be expected to have some of the emotional problems that they naturally have at some times, but it is by no means a permanent state. A few, however, are at risk of going right off the rails and giving and getting five years or so of absolute hell. Adolescents are people; they come in all shapes and sizes, and all have their funny little ways. It's just that some have more than others.

Stages of adolescence

It's helpful to divide adolescence into three distinct sections: early, middle and late. They correspond quite well to secondary school age groups and don't seem to be strongly related to stages of puberty.

Early adolescence (Ages 11 to 14, UK school years 7 to 9, US school grades 6 to 8)

The start of early adolescence usually brings big changes with it. Your lovely young ten-year-old can turn into a moody and argumentative eleven-year-old. At other times, they can revert to their previous loving selves and be clingy, particularly in the earlier stages. This will more often be with the same-sex parent.

If you're not aware of the almost universal nature of the changes, it can take you very much by surprise and you start to wonder what you are doing wrong. The simple answer to that is that you are probably doing things pretty much right. It is your child who is off track. Having said that, there is plenty you can do and we'll deal with this in later chapters.

At this stage, adolescents begin to want much more independence, which they are not yet ready for. They might have extreme temper tantrums that exceed even those of the 'terrible twos' and adolescents can be quite offensive (in the heat of the moment) and tell you just how stupid they think you are. They may also even be embarrassed to be seen with you at times.

Girls usually prefer to have a small group of close friends, but occasionally it's just one friend from whom they are inseparable. There is usually a larger group of mates as well. Boys generally prefer to have one best friend and a larger group of mates. These friends and the closer mates provide not only friendship but also a sense of identity away from the seemingly increasingly stupid adults in their lives.

The desire to be as much like their friends as possible can lead to extremes of fashion, hairstyles and musical taste. This is typical herd mentality and allegiance to the herd can be extreme. Anyone not 'in' the herd is most definitely 'out', and this, of course, includes you. Other people's points of view are not worth considering if they are not in complete agreement with the herd's ideas and name-calling is standard practice. The variety of offensive terms that youngsters have for others not like themselves is astounding.

What is often referred to as risk-taking often starts at this stage. That basically means that teenagers start to do things that they know are pretty stupid, but they do them anyway. This means that tobacco and alcohol (common drugs in the adult world) look attractive and recreational drug use becomes a distinctly attractive option. Basically, anything forbidden becomes appealing no matter how risky.

Both at home and at school, and in the wider world, values and rules are always questioned. The boundaries are sometimes pushed much harder than common sense would advise. But common sense is uncommon at this age and advice is rarely welcomed, much less taken. Any kind of attention is better than no attention, even that which causes pain.

This is called self-defeating behaviour, and many teenagers seem to be addicted to it. They know perfectly well that certain types of behaviour are going to get a painful response, but they go ahead and do it anyway. It's well known that being cheeky to an already angry person isn't going to get you what you really want, but isn't that exactly what most teenagers do?

Around this time there is a widening in the ability gap between the most and least able at school. The most able youngsters find that their increasing brainpower is starting to pay off. The least able seem to learn only helplessness. Sometimes these youngsters find that the only success that seems possible is notoriety, so it is actively sought and often found.

By fourteen years old or so both boys and girls are starting to think that they are now fully adult. They want all the freedoms that other adults have. When these freedoms are refused, they can react strongly. Their ideas of how real people resolve differences are influenced more by the antics of over-dramatic soap opera characters than by the philosophy of Mahatma Ghandi.

Teenage thinking skills are confined to their own direct experience which, in itself, is limited. Things are always either right or wrong – and you don't need me to tell you who is always right. Life is full of give and take – and you know who does the taking. Blame can always be laid for everything that goes wrong – and you can easily guess where the blame can never fall.

Middle adolescence (Ages 15 to 16, UK school years 10 and 11, US school grades 9 and 10)

By this stage, most adolescents will discover sex and that opposites attract. It is still a time for hanging out with friends, but there is often a deep attachment to a boyfriend or girlfriend. Some will go from one to another with a speed that leaves you breathless, a few will form long-term relationships that are going to be 'forever' or even longer. The middle adolescent's heart is frequently broken and, for them, this can be utterly traumatic.

Their emerging sexuality isn't yet coupled with mature emotions and they confuse intimacy with sex. They can see that the two are related, but often imagine that if the sex comes first, the intimacy will follow. We adults know that the only formula for a fulfilling relationship is intimacy followed by sex. This ordering problem is very much compounded by TV, films, popular songs, and so forth, which glamorize sex and use it as a commodity.

Relationships with younger brothers and sisters can become strained and create an almost constant atmosphere at this time. This seems to be especially true between sisters and a constant bickering can fill the household. It can also be a time of intense conflict with the same-sex parent.

Friendships start to become based on common interests at this time and as new friends are made, former ones often fall by the wayside.

Their thinking skills are developing quite nicely by now and they may become attached to causes. This is typically the time that an intense religious fervour develops, or a commitment to veganism or something similar. Many are starting to move away from the herd mentality and starting to question things for themselves. They start to get the idea that being different doesn't automatically mean being bad and they start to appreciate that there are shades of grey between the black and white of a couple of years ago.

The downside to these improving thinking skills is that parents' beliefs and standards can be questioned more closely than ever. This is great for the adolescent and tiring and challenging for the parents. A typical example would be parents' insistence on a midweek bedtime of 10 p.m. and getting up at 7 a.m. The adolescent can then say, 'Hang on. This is my body and if I want to stay up later and get up later and go to school without breakfast then I will.' Sexual activity is an even greater minefield. Parents and other adults advise restraint. Popular culture screams otherwise.

It's crunch time academically. Those that are going to succeed start to make a commitment to success and can get really focused on schoolwork. Those who can see little hope of academic success or little point in it can give up completely. Most of the teenagers in the middle of the academic achievement range have little idea how to get better grades and just coast along.

It can also be a time of great stress. Most will realize that what they do at school over the next two years will have a strong influence on how their lives can progress. There can be the stress of living up to their own or their parents' dreams. There can also be the stress of seeing a life of mediocrity if results aren't as good as they should be. Sexual orientation can also become a worry at this stage.

Occasionally, there can be a complete loss of faith in anything good and worthwhile. If failure in school and socially becomes a habit, then there doesn't seem to be much point in the adolescent mind. This can be a sad and desperately serious situation.

Late adolescence (Ages 17 to 20, UK school years 12+, US school grades 11+)

By now, teenagers are becoming much more adult in their appearance and behaviour. They are beginning to understand their parents much better and relating to their peers and other adults in a rational and sensible fashion. There is still some way to go before mature thinking patterns become established, but they are nearly there.

By far the greatest danger to this age group is that they are still taking risks. This still means that they are likely to be drinking alcohol and may be using recreational drugs. Neither of these is health-enhancing. But the greatest danger to life and limb comes from cars and motorcycles. The insurance companies are right. Young drivers are quite simply a huge danger to themselves and others on the roads.

Full adulthood is in sight.

It ain't that simple

Just as physical development depends to an extent on nutrition and physical and environmental factors, the same is true for emotional development. Whilst every adolescent will complete all the stages of puberty, some will not fully develop emotionally. It's a sad fact that a significant minority of adults are still emotionally immature.

It's our job as parents to create the right emotional atmosphere to allow our youngsters to develop as fully as they can. This means an atmosphere of love and understanding, certainly, but there is much more than that. Love and understanding by themselves are not enough. We need to make certain that they are translated into practical actions.

That's the way it is

In an earlier career, I used to do family research. This often involved looking up information in old local newspapers. I was amazed to find that many of the articles in old papers were almost identical to stories in my local paper today. Youths have been fighting in the streets and getting drunk at parties for about as long as streets and parties have been around. Even Aristotle and Plato had plenty to say about the vagaries of youth.

Nothing that you, I, or anyone else can do is ever going to change these things. Adolescents are adolescents and will do the things that adolescents do and always have done. They cannot do anything different – they are simply living out the script that biology and our complex society has laid down for them.

We need to make sure that we can survive the adolescent years without being irreparably damaged by our teenagers. We need to make sure that our teenagers can survive the adolescent years without being irreparably damaged by us. We're the adults. It's up to us to have the adult attitudes and to do the adult things that will ensure everyone's survival.

Review

- Puberty refers to the physical changes that children undergo on the way to adulthood. Boys and girls start puberty at slightly different times, but this is about the time they start secondary school. Puberty is usually completed by the time high school is finished. During this period they undergo enormous physical and emotional changes.
- Adolescence refers to the emotional and intellectual changes that children undergo on the way to adulthood. Not all children complete all the stages of emotional and intellectual maturity. Some get stuck at lower levels and never develop into full adulthood.
- Adolescence is a fact of life and adolescents have always caused problems for themselves and others. Your teenager is normal.

Action Exercises

- Have sympathy and empathy. Teenagers are going through emotional turmoil. Be understanding and go with the flow of emotions. Be very supportive.

- Be aware of the stages of adolescent development. Adapt your behaviour and attitudes to suit the growing development of your adolescent teenager.

TWO

Teenagers' Thinking Problems

Start with the end in mind

Teenagers misbehave and get obnoxious on occasions simply because of the way that they think. The problem is that their thinking strategies and processes are immature and incomplete. They are neither the sweet and innocent childlike thoughts of yesteryear, nor are they the adult, logical thought-patterns of the not-too-distant future. An understanding of the nature of this thinking goes a long way to explaining quite a lot.

It is also reassuring. Teenagers behave and think like teenagers simply because they *are* teenagers. It is nothing personal toward you and your adolescent is more than likely normal and there is nothing to worry about. There is simply a change in their biology and their behaviour is a direct consequence of that. Your teenager will most likely become a responsible and loveable adult in time. It's the time factor that is the problem. Can you both survive it with sanity and family relationships intact?

There are three things that we need to understand.

■ Teenagers' brains are undergoing a change. This is thought to be due in part to the hormones which their bodies are producing and in part to a fine-tuning of their brain structure.

15

- Teenagers are learning how to think for themselves. No amount of thinking for them is going to work; they simply have to do it for themselves. You have heard the old saying 'There's many a slip twixt cup and lip'. Well, there's many a mistaken thought on the way to good thinking. I can guarantee that your teenager can be relied upon to have most of them at one time or another.

- Adolescence isn't a single stage in life. It is just a convenient term used to describe a part of the continuous changes that we all go through between childhood and adulthood. In particular, teenagers go through a moral development which may be roughly described as going from selfishness to selflessness.

Teenage brains

It used to be thought that the human brain was just about complete by age six or seven and that there was little change that took place after that. This is now known to be quite false. As brain-imaging technology has developed, it's now possible to see which parts of the brain work hard during thinking. The functions, if not the workings, of most parts of the brain are well understood by now, so we can know what is going on.

Teenagers' brains undergo an upgrade and rewiring process from the age of about eleven to the early twenties. The process is similar to what happens at about age two. No new brain cells grow, but the brain grows billions of new connections between cells. The connections that are used regularly become stronger. The ones that are unused are pruned back.

There are obvious implications here for intellectual development. If an adolescent spends time learning new things, playing sports and having fun, those brain circuits will be strengthened. Life-long learning and fitness become a part of life. If time is spent watching TV and in non-productive time-wasting, those brain circuits will be strengthened.

Just as certain circuits in your house would be out of operation during rewiring, certain thinking circuits don't work as well as they did before, or as they will when the process is finished. Understanding this helps you understand why teenagers are the way that they are. The major functions which are impaired are:

1.   understanding the emotions of other people; and
2.   rational thinking.

Add to that the hormone swings that their bodies and brains are experiencing and you have a recipe for a few years of upset.

Understanding the emotions of other people

Adults understand the emotional signals of other people using the frontal cortex of the brain. This area is responsible for the highest order thinking skills. Teenagers use a more primitive part of the brain called the amygdala which is associated more with instinctive reaction. (The amygdala is

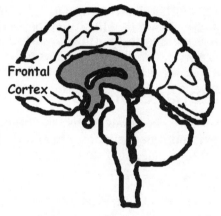

buried deep in the brain's limbic system, shaded on the diagram.) Where adults and younger children are able to identify people's emotions very accurately, teenagers lose this ability. What this means is that when you give your teenager a hard stare that would shrivel an adult, your teenager wonders why you have a funny look on your face and what your problem is.

You have to make your feelings, thoughts, wants, needs and emotions very plain and unambiguous to a teenager. This means that you have to be assertive and encourage rational thought rather than gut reactions.

Rational thinking

Planning and thinking through the consequences of actions are also done in the developing frontal cortex. This doesn't mean that teenagers cannot think rational thoughts. But it does mean that teenagers find it more difficult to do their rational thinking on the hoof. When you ask your teen, 'What on Earth possessed you to do that?' and you get the answer, 'Dunno', or 'It seemed like a good idea at the time', it's the truth. She simply doesn't know because she didn't make a rational decision. And she didn't do so because she couldn't do so. Teenagers need a lot of help with this area.

Stinking thinking

The technical term for this is cognitive distortions. This simply means that the thinking (= cognitive) process is out of alignment with the truth (= distorted). Teenagers are subject to a whole host of these errors in thinking, but there are four which seem to be universal and dangerous and a fifth which is very prevalent and destructive.

1. I am the centre of the universe.
2. I am unique.
3. The rules don't apply to me.
4. I am immortal.
5. Good is bad and bad is good.

These errors are mainly based on the well-known adolescent egocentrism which leads to two types of thought. The first one is called the Imaginary Audience, which refers to the adolescent belief that everybody is as interested in them as they are in themselves. The second one is called the Personal Fable, which refers to the adolescent belief that they are unique in the history of the world.

I am the centre of the universe

Edward Hubble (after whom the famous space telescope was named) discovered that the universe is expanding. Cosmologists are still debating whether the universe has an identifiable centre or not. But one thing is for sure: if a centre is ever discovered, it won't be a teenager.

This idea is based on the Imaginary Audience type of thought. The logic seems to be: 'I am important to me. Therefore, I am important to everybody.' This brings about an

RENT-A-TEEN

Teenagers available for work: baby minding; yard clearance; shopping; gardening etc.

GET ONE NOW
WHILE THEY STILL
KNOW
EVERYTHING

Reasonable daily and half-daily rates

exaggerated idea of their own importance. They have the idea that everybody is in awe of them and spends all their time thinking about them and their wonderful ways. In particular, they imagine that everyone else is impressed by their cool. This is why teenagers feel the need to show off in front of mates and make a lot of noise.

Because some adolescents get locked in to this type of thinking, they cannot see that most other people don't really care for their loud and aggressive behaviour. You and I know that courtesy is much more impressive than cool. Try telling that to a teenager!

I am unique

This is an example of the Personal Fable. Since they are unique, no one else could possibly understand the way they feel and think. Their uniqueness helps them in any argument. No matter what, nobody, and especially an adult, could have their particular experience or specialist knowledge. The sense of uniqueness is aided by the Imaginary Audience. Since other people are focused entirely on them, they *must* be unique.

This can lead to the utmost depths of despair at times. When things go wrong, as they often do in life, they can be so wrong that there is no possible solution imaginable. Nobody else could ever have experienced such misery and survived unscathed; or so they think.

The rules don't apply to me

This is another direct consequence of the Personal Fable. Teenagers realize that rules exist, but because of their uniqueness, imagine that the rules are solely there to protect them from others. Thus, no one may touch your daughter's things, but she may rifle through Mum's drawers for a pair of tights. You'll often hear: 'I know my rights!' Less frequent is: 'I recognize and fulfil my responsibilities'.

I am immortal

The same Personal Fable idea is applied to personal safety. In this instance, it is: 'You are stupid and put yourself in danger. I am cool and can come to no harm'. This covers everything from skateboarding without a helmet to unprotected sex. Teenagers get plenty of personal, social and health education, but they truly believe that the dangers are not for them. They are far better educated about the wisdom and foolishness of many personal, social and health issues than we parents ever were, but still nothing is changing.

There has not been a noticeable change in teenagers' personal, social or health habits over the past few years. Their belief in their own immortality is the sole cause. Education may be changing, but basic biology isn't.

Good is bad and bad is good

This particular error has at least two alternative forms:

- It's smart to be dumb and it's dumb to be smart.
- Failure is success and success is failure.

Everybody longs for success and admiration. This is no less true for teenagers than for anyone else. If real academic or sports success isn't a realistic option, then it is better to choose to succeed in failing. This does seem to be almost a standard part of some sub-cultures. Even in the lower years of primary school, 'swot' is a term of abuse alongside 'teacher's pet' and 'nerd'. My oldest son, when he was in primary school, was verbally attacked with 'Yahhh. Your dad's smart.' Happily, he didn't take it in the way it was intended.

Correcting stinking thinking

Our role as parents has to be to guide our teenagers away from this stinking thinking and towards the truth. The technical term for this is cognitive realignment. That is to say, that thinking needs to be aligned with reality. Personal and peer myths and legends aren't a good basis on which to build a life. We adults live in the real world and need to help our teenagers see at least some of the details.

Whenever you hear an example of this 'stinking thinking' you should question it deeply. Ask them, 'Do you really think that?' Your teenager should be able to see that it is wrong thinking and will probably be able to come up with something more appropriate. It will certainly take time, but that's the one thing that you have plenty of – five years or more. The more help and encouragement that can be given and received, the happier and smoother will be the experience of the teenage years, both for you and your teenager.

Stages of thinking development

A psychologist named Jean Piaget studied the moral development of young children from the 1930s to the 1960s. Basically, he discovered that youngsters develop their ideas based on deciding what is and isn't fair. In the earlier stages, the guiding question is: 'What is fair for me?' Later the question becomes: 'What is fair for everybody?'

Piaget's work was extended by Lawrence Kohlberg in the 1960s and 1970s. Kohlberg studied the way in which moral thought developed from childhood to adulthood. He identified six stages of moral reasoning divided into three levels. They describe a progressive growth from childish selfishness to adult selflessness.

The three levels are called:

1. Pre-conventional (= selfishness);
2. Conventional (= acceptance); and
3. Post-conventional (= selflessness).

Pre-conventional (= selfishness)

The driving force at this level is obeying the rules to avoid punishment. This is simply because the consequences of not doing so are unpleasant. The rules are simply handed down and enforced by parents or the school. If there is no one around to enforce the rules, then they don't really exist at that time.

Gradually, the idea of 'fairness' creeps in, but it is still selfish. The idea is that my actions can affect the way that you behave towards me. As long as I am fair towards you, you should be fair towards me – that's only fair. It also works the other way. If you are unfair to me, then I shall be unfair towards you. You hit me, I'll hit you. That's fair. Self-control is not really understood.

Conventional (= acceptance)

At this stage, there is more awareness of the importance of groups and that rules are there to help groups function. There's family, and the family identity depends on certain rules being followed. There's society in general, and society's rules are there to protect everybody. Rules are there to be obeyed just because they make everybody's life easier and more pleasant.

There is a danger at this stage. Youngsters are becoming increasingly aware that there is a price to be paid for everything. Social acceptance means paying the price of socially acceptable behaviour. But for much of the time, they are being told to pay the price without being told what they are buying. This is often true in school. They know that the price is that rules have to be obeyed, but for what?

At this stage, there is self-control. Just because you hit me doesn't mean that I have to hit you. I know that hitting is wrong and never solves anything.

Post-conventional (= selflessness)

At this level, the rules are thought about in much more general terms. There is an emerging idea that there are absolutes of right and wrong and that these are more important than any single rule. It's an emerging personal

22

morality based on the highest of principles. I do the right things for no other reason than they are the right things to do. Of course, this also opens up the idea of not obeying standard rules if they don't fit the individual's morality. There are some gender differences at this level. Males tend to make their rules based on principles. Females tend to make their rules based on social justice.

Just because you hit me doesn't mean that I have to hit you. I have choices and the ability to make those choices. I may decide not to hit you because there is really no benefit in it. However, if it will prevent you hitting me again or hitting someone else, then I will. I may even decide to hit you first if it will prevent you hitting other people. Hmm. I have a moral dilemma here.

Juvenile delinquency

There are many causes of juvenile delinquency ranging from learning difficulties to extreme social deprivation, and we can't hope to deal with them all here. But we can note two important findings. First of all, a good proportion of younger delinquents simply don't realize that their behaviour is unacceptable. Secondly, the vast majority of them avoid delinquent behaviour if they think that they will be found out.

I believe that this makes things quite clear. Delinquent behaviour is largely a function of pre-conventional thinking. We all know that it is common and we all know that it often passes with time. You must know many people of your own age who were wild teenagers and have grown into perfectly decent adults. It's helping your teenager reach the third stage that will overcome most problems. They simply cannot reach adulthood without it.

It ain't that simple

We've got to remember that we are dealing with complex people here. We all know from experience that any adult can be as nice as pie one day and be grumpy the next day. You can have a laugh and a joke sometimes, at other times it just doesn't work. Teenagers are even more variable than the touchiest of adults. Their moods can swing from being joyful and creative one moment to being in the depths of despair the next.

Growth is not a simple straight-line thing. It couldn't possibly be. There are just too many factors affecting it. Not only factors such as physical and emotional development, but factors outside of anyone's control. Your adolescent might be having problems at school or be going through a romantic disaster. No matter what it is, it will have an effect.

There is always going to be an argument about which is more important: nature or nurture. The truth is that both have their role to play. Fortunately, nature is benign. Our main concern is that we can nurture our children along the way and help determine, to some extent, what sort of adults they become. That is exactly the point of this chapter and Chapter One. If you have a sympathetic understanding of what adolescence involves, you can adapt your nurture to the nature of your special adolescent.

Review

In the quest to help our teenagers develop responsibility, we need to succeed in three areas.

- Firstly, we need to help them use their brains as well as they can. They need to be taught to look for emotional signals and to learn what these signals mean. They also need a lot of help with decision making. Until the needs of others are considered, and rational and reasoned decisions can be made quickly and reliably, responsibility is not possible.
- Secondly, we must help them develop a realization that their stinking thinking is not realistic. The world just doesn't operate in that way. Responsibility and egocentricity cannot exist together.
- Thirdly, we need to help them along the moral development path and get them to post-conventional (= selfless) thinking. It is quite impossible to be successful in life without reaching this stage.

Action Exercises

■ Help your teenagers become more aware of the emotions and needs of other people. Help them develop empathy by modelling it yourself.

■ Make your communication clear. If you want something, ask for it clearly. If you have a particular feeling about something, make it clear. Don't even attempt to use subtlety. It simply won't work.

■ Watch out for 'stinking thinking'. Gently guide your teenager to an understanding that others' needs are just as important as their own.

■ Be aware of your teenager's moral development and constantly guide them gently towards the next level.

THREE

Communication Skills

Start with the end in mind

There was once a farmer who had an orphaned bull-calf. It was a fine animal and the farmer didn't want to lose it. He had to take the calf from the field and into the barn where he could look after it. He led the calf out of the field easily enough and was nearly at the barn when the calf took fright and rooted itself to the spot.

The farmer heaved on the rope around the calf's neck. The calf didn't budge. The farmer put his shoulder to the calf's rump and pushed with all his might. The calf didn't budge. The farmer yelled and hit the calf with his stick. The calf didn't budge. The farmer jumped up and down with rage and cursed and screamed and shouted. The calf didn't budge.

The farmer's wife was in the kitchen and standing at the window looking at the spectacle and shaking her head in disbelief. She came out into the yard, wiping her hands on her pinafore and came up to the calf. She spoke to it gently and stroked its head. She put her face close to the calf's face, placed an arm around its neck, and nuzzled it, all the while speaking softly and gently.

Then she placed her thumb in the calf's mouth and the calf started to suckle. She gently withdrew her thumb and the calf moved forward to take it again. The wife started to withdraw her thumb again, but this time the calf moved forwards with it. Thus, the farmer's wife led the calf into the barn. There she gave the calf a bottle of milk.

As she came out, her husband looked at her in disbelief and wonderment. 'Don't look at me like that,' said his wife. 'It was easy enough. You were thinking about what you wanted. I was thinking about what the calf wanted.'

No need for conflict

Your teenager wants more freedom and responsibility. You want your teenager to have more freedom and responsibility. Your teenager wants to have fun. You want your teenager to have fun. Your teenager doesn't want to get hurt. You don't want your teenager to get hurt. There is much more space for agreement than for disagreement.

We usually get into conflict not because of a lack of love, but because we get frustrated and take the easiest way out. This is, of course, to start bullying, shouting, and laying down the law. This is the approach that others usually take with us and it gets results. That it doesn't get good results doesn't occur to most people.

You know for yourself that you don't like to be bullied and shouted at and made to feel small and powerless. Well, neither does your teenager. You also know that you can easily be persuaded to do things if you can see that there are benefits for you and others. Your teenager is exactly the same. Teenagers may take a little more persuading and guidance, but they are, essentially, no different from you and me.

Conflict is absolutely guaranteed to fail to produce long-term peace. It doesn't work in the Middle East or in Northern Ireland or in any other trouble spot and it won't work in your home (or your teenager's school) either. The only route to peace and harmony is through listening to the other person's point of view and talking sensibly and sensitively.

It's not an easy call, and no one is pretending that it is. Very few people are skilled communicators in business and commerce, much less at home with the family. It isn't something that is generally taught. We have the idea that the only way to get what you want is to go out and take it. It's the playground mentality – and it doesn't work.

27

Choose your ego

Way back in 1964, Eric Berne, an expatriate Canadian living in San Francisco, published a book called *Games People Play*. This book introduced the ideas of Transactional Analysis (TA) to the world. TA became the popular psychology of the 1960s, 1970s and 1980s. It has largely been overtaken these days by other therapies, but it still has some useful lessons to teach. A lot of the language is still in use today.

Berne noticed that people behaved in different ways according to the situation that they were in. He also noticed that some people were stuck in certain behaviour patterns. He classified behaviour as coming from one of three ego states. People could be in a CHILD, ADULT or PARENT state. They are written in capital letters to avoid confusion with a real person. This is what people are talking about when advising you to 'get in touch with your inner child'.

(What follows is an adaptation of Berne's theory. I have changed and simplified things a great deal to refer only to avoiding and settling conflict.)

ADULT is an undivided state. It's neutral, unemotional and logical. Think Spock and you've got it. PARENT can be in either of two states: HAPPY PARENT or ANGRY PARENT. Similarly, CHILD can be HAPPY CHILD or ANGRY CHILD. Remember that these are states and not people. You know for yourself that you can be ADULT at some times and CHILD at others. Your boss probably spends quite a lot of time at work in PARENT. Even young children can be in PARENT with younger children and be ADULT amongst themselves.

So we've all got five possible ego states. Any person can be in any of the five states depending on the situation. Generally, your state will suit the situation you find yourself in. You'll be happy or angry depending on the emotions flying about at the time. If there are no strong emotions, you'll probably be in ADULT.

If you care to do the maths, you'll find that there are theoretically twenty-five possible pairings of ego states that two people can use. Most of them are not possible in reality. In any case, we are only interested in avoiding and handling conflict situations.

There are three pairings of states that can communicate at length.

Ego states

HAPPY PARENT	ANGRY PARENT
ADULT	
HAPPY CHILD	ANGRY CHILD

HAPPY PARENT ↔ HAPPY CHILD

No problems here. All is sweetness and light and everyone is happy. This is the way that most of your communication was when your child was small and utterly delightful. This is the kind of communication that you want to be having much of the time – even with your teenager.

ADULT ↔ ADULT

No problem here. It may not be sweetness and light, but it's businesslike and constructive. The conversation can continue and the job gets done. This is the kind of communication that your teenager will be wanting. As adolescence progresses towards adulthood there'll be more and more of this type of communication.

ANGRY PARENT ↔ ANGRY CHILD

Not nice! You can row for hours or even days on end if you want to. It's communication, but it's not positive or helpful and doesn't leave anyone feeling good about it. Problems never get solved in this kind of situation and no one comes out of it with much dignity or respect for the other. This is what you really need to avoid.

There are two types of communication that cannot possibly continue at length.

ANGRY PARENT ↔ HAPPY CHILD; HAPPY PARENT ↔ ANGRY CHILD

You know from experience that these just don't happen. And this gives the clue as to how you can control communications with your teenager to make sure that they are positive and constructive.

If you are in ANGRY PARENT, you almost force your teenager to respond from ANGRY CHILD. You create a row. Teenagers just rise to the bait. If you issue a challenge, it's like a red rag to a bull. Teenagers are just longing for opportunities to flex their muscles and hold their own – and here you are providing them with the perfect opportunity to go head-to-head with you. The lesson is obvious – keep your temper.

If your teenager comes to you in ANGRY CHILD mode, you are almost forced to respond from ANGRY PARENT. But wait a moment! You are the adult and you have choices. If you refuse to be drawn, you can choose to reply from either the ADULT or HAPPY PARENT state.

One of two things will happen. Either your teenager will stomp off in a temper, frustrated that the row didn't happen or they will switch into a complementary state. If your teenager is disagreeable and stomps off in a temper, it's not your problem. By keeping your temper and your dignity, you have agreed to disagree. But there is always the possibility that your teenager will change into the complementary state. So if you are in ADULT and your adolescent is in ANGRY CHILD, they might switch to ADULT to carry on the discussion. On the other hand, if you can hold the HAPPY PARENT state for long enough, your adolescent will automatically switch into HAPPY CHILD. The lesson is obvious; and it's the same lesson as before – keep your temper.

I'm not saying that you cannot be strict and forceful at times. There are always times when you have to be. But you need to do it in a way that maintains dignity for everyone – you and your teenager. That means ADULT ↔ ADULT. I'm saying that you need to avoid anyone being out of control.

You already know that you cannot beat someone into agreeing with you and that conflict is counter-productive. The only way to avoid conflict is not create it yourself and to refuse to be drawn into it when it is offered to you.

Learning to listen

Most people think that communication means talking. And most people are wrong. Communication means listening, and listening in a way that is going to get you the information that you want and need. You cannot possibly hope to influence someone and help them to grow just by talking. Most experts on communication recommend the 70–30 rule. Listen for 70 per cent of the time and speak for 30 per cent. I prefer to note that you were born with two ears and one mouth. I recommend that you use them in that proportion.

Do you remember your first true love? Do you remember how you used to spend hours and hours just talking? You would spill out all your ideas and bare your soul. You had wild, crazy ideas about the world and how you saw it and shared them openly and without fear. Can you remember how it felt to have someone hanging on your every word? Do you remember how you used to feel loved and affirmed simply by being listened to? That is the joy of speaking to an empathic listener. Wouldn't you like your teenager to feel that joy with you?

Your teenager has got lots of things to say and needs someone who is going to listen to them. That person has got to be you. Most of the things you hear will be right, some of them will be wrong, and some of them will be somewhere in between and rather confused. It's your job as a parent to listen to all of it and help your teenager. Affirm and encourage the good thinking and help to adjust the wrong and confused thinking.

It's not a difficult thing to do. All you need is to dedicate a little time and a lot of love to developing a deep relationship. The key idea as Stephen Covey puts it is, 'Seek first to understand, then to be understood'. It's not enough to feel the love: you have to show it as well.

Empathic listening is listening, not from your own world-view, but from your teenager's world-view. It means trying to get inside your teenager's head, heart and very soul, and you can only do this when you are deeply in rapport with someone. You have to abandon yourself and all your own preconceived ideas and opinions and accept fully that your teenager has opinions and ideas that are deeply important.

To do this you have to become aware of body language as well as spoken language. Notice how your teenager is sitting, and sit in the same way. Listen carefully to the language your teenager is using and try to use the same sort of language. Adjust how fast you speak to match your teenager's speed and even adjust the tone of voice and loudness to match. A useful technique here is called the echo technique. You rephrase or even repeat word for word what is said so that you make sure that you understand completely. Smile and nod often and make affirming noises.

Without prompting from you, your teenager will start to ask the questions that really need answering. Once your teenager really feels understood, there will be a deep need inside to understand you.

This all seems difficult at first, but after a few minutes a wonderful thing begins to happen. As the two of you get more and more into rapport and more into the communication, it just flows and both your hearts open up. It is just a natural part of human relationships and is programmed into us. All we really have to do is to create the opportunity for it to happen – and happen it will.

How do you know that someone loves you? It's when the other person lets you know in lots of little ways and a few really big ways that you are loved. How does your teenager know love? It's exactly the same. There is a certain magic about being listened to and affirmed that we don't get nearly often enough. It's loving, being loved and feeling at one with the other person. It's a delightful and deeply meaningful experience for both of you and is one you shouldn't miss.

You can't learn empathy from a book. You learn empathy by being and doing. And deep empathic listening is the route to developing it as a natural part of your family life.

Assertiveness

It would be wonderful if you could expect complete co-operation all the time. But this is the real world and, if you have an adolescent in the family, you know full well that it isn't going to happen that way. There are always going to be times when you need to be firm and lay down the law. You need to be able to do it so that everybody feels good about it.

The only way to do this effectively is to do it assertively. Assertiveness is *not* about bullying. It is about being open, honest, and entirely adult and, as the Desiderata puts it, stating your truth quietly. You will know when you are assertive. You will get more of what you want with less stress and less backchat.

Just as assertiveness is not about bullying, it is equally about not allowing yourself to be bullied. This means that you need to be able to state quite clearly and sometimes quite forcibly that you expect certain standards to be met. It means that you can state that there are certain types of behaviour which are completely unacceptable and which will not be tolerated. Both of these need to be done in such a way as to make it much more likely that you will get the co-operation that you want without making anybody feel bad about you.

You can do this by giving all the right signals. These signals are the words, tone of voice, and body language you use. They all have to work together in such a way as to show that you are quite serious about the message you are giving.

Your words have to be constructive, positive and respectful and use 'I' language rather than 'you' language.

Always make sure that you say what you **DO** want rather than what you **DON'T** want.

- ☑ I'd like you to wear your slippers in the house.
- ☒ I don't want you to wear your shoes in the house.
- ☒ You mustn't wear your shoes in the house.

The first one is positive and respectful and contains an embedded command 'wear your slippers in the house'. The second one actually contains the words 'wear your shoes in the house' which is giving an embedded command to do exactly what you don't want. The third one is 'you' language and contains the same embedded command.

Always talk about the behaviour and not the person and say what you want, not what you don't want.

- ☑ I would prefer that you speak to me politely and quietly.
- ☒ I would prefer it if you didn't swear and shout at me.
- ☒ Don't speak to me in that way.
- ☒ You are being very rude. Or, You are rude.

The first one is stating clearly what you want. The second and third contain embedded commands to do what you don't want. The fourth is describing the person, and this is always destructive. When this type of message is being given time after time, day in and day out, your teenager isn't going to be helped to develop a positive and constructive self-image.

When making requests it helps to make the reasons behind them clear.

☑ I'd like you to help me clear the table so I can get the washing up done early.

☑ It would be really helpful if you have your shower now so I can get mine.

It helps to acknowledge that some things you say might not meet with immediate agreement.

☑ I know that you might see things differently, but I feel that bedtimes are important on school nights.

It also helps to prepare the ground.

☑ I'd like you to think about this carefully.

Acknowledge differences openly.

☑ Yes, Mandy's parents might let her stay up until 11.30, but we both know that it isn't sensible or helpful to Mandy.

Use 'and' instead of 'but' whenever possible. 'And' shows agreement and that there is more to be considered. 'But' shows disagreement.

☑ Yes, you want to go out, and you haven't finished your homework yet.

☒ Yes, you want to go out, but you haven't finished your homework yet.

They have subtly different meanings, haven't they? The first one is likely to get a much better response because it invites the conversation to continue. The second one is just begging for an argument.

Go for Win-Win

There are frequently times when things aren't as clear-cut as they could be and there needs to be a discussion to get things sorted out. This could be a recipe for an argument. There is one certain outcome of any argument. Everybody loses. This may not always be obvious, but it is nonetheless true for that. Look at it this way, no one likes to lose an argument. If you lose an argument, how do you feel about the person who won it? Do you feel positive or negative towards them? The answer is that you always feel negative.

If you win an argument, how do you feel? It's tempting to feel a certain glow of pride at beating someone, even your own children. 'Ha,' you think, 'She'll think twice before crossing me again. I showed her who is the boss around here.' But will she think twice? And who is the boss? Who bossed you into the argument in the first place?

Have you ever known an argument that prevents arguments? Arguments become addictive and teenagers simply cannot resist a good one. They are desperate to try flexing their muscles, and the only way to flex those arguing muscles is to get plenty of practice arguing. These things spiral and can get out of control.

And even if you do feel a sense of satisfaction from winning, do you feel that your relationship should be based on having winners and losers on the same team? If you win the argument, you lose the relationship. If you lose the argument, you lose the relationship. Win or lose, you lose.

The simple answer is, don't have arguments. Go for a situation in which everybody is a winner. Go for Win-Win.

It requires a certain mindset that may come as a novelty to your teenager (who probably sees conflict as the only way of sorting out differences). The mindset is that everybody wants much the same things and has the ability to be flexible and creative to get what everybody wants. You both need to have the flexibility to realize that what you want in the end may not be the same as what you thought you wanted in the first place.

	I lose ☹	I win ☺
You win ☺	I lose You win	I win You win
You lose ☹	I lose You lose	I win You lose

This is quite different from a negotiation in which both people lose something in order to gain less than they wanted. Win-Win situations are those in which you both get what you know to be the best for both of you and relationships are maintained and strengthened.

Families can always find Win-Win if they really want to. It's easy to do because everyone in the family really wants the same thing. Everyone wants to be happy and successful and help make everybody else happy.

Everybody is respectful. No one raises their voice or bullies anyone. Everyone speaks politely and states what they want in mild terms. There is no shouting, name calling, threatening or any other form of out-of-control behaviour. Everybody is reasonable. Everybody wants to be democratic and have their hopes, wants and desires attended to without trampling other people's rights. Everybody is affirmed. Everybody is made to feel important and a loved and valuable member of the family. Certainly, the parents have power of authority, but it is a benign authority and used for the benefit of all.

I win – You win
We are both happy with the outcome. We have both got the good things that we want and have avoided the bad things that we really don't want. Our relationship is affirmed.

I win – You lose
We have an argument about something. I use my authority in order to beat you down. There is a danger that I can feel good and powerful in this. You will feel powerless, resentful and bitter. Our relationship is damaged.

I lose – You win
We have an argument. You manage to wear me down and get your way despite my protestations. You feel victorious, I feel angry and frustrated. Our relationship is damaged.

I lose – You lose
We have an argument. Neither of us wins. You don't get what you want and I don't get what I want. Our relationship is very seriously damaged since we both feel powerless and resent that the other will not give way.

Getting the job done

Sometimes the agreement will be that your teenager undertakes to do a particular task or makes a regular commitment like homework or household chores. The question then becomes how to make sure that the job gets done. After all, there's little point in coming to agreements of any type unless they bear fruit. You want to help your teenager succeed as soon as possible. Then there's a good, strong base to build further successes on.

You can help your teenager on the road to success quite easily. Simply ask: 'Do you need any help from me to get the job done?'

Offer practical help and emotional support. If your teenager recognizes that it might present a bit of a challenge, you might be asked for help. Your teenager may say that there is no need for help. In this case, give reassurance that you'll be delighted to help out if it's needed at some time.

Emotional bank account

Stephen Covey describes every family member having an emotional bank account with everybody else. As long as everybody makes good deposits of love and positive behaviour into everybody else's accounts, the odd withdrawal of negative behaviour every so often is easily covered. We all have our funny little moments at times. The secret is to have them infrequently, and always to be making deposits and saving for a rainy day.

When these things are in place, there is very little opportunity for bad feelings. Of course, everybody has their moments and not all is going to be perfect. Everybody loses their rag from time to time. As long as the emotional bank account is well in credit, these withdrawals can be covered. The overall atmosphere is overwhelmingly positive and supportive and the odd glitch isn't going to do any lasting harm.

Now *that's* a rich family.

Review

- There is never any need for conflict. You can avoid most of it by remaining cool, calm and collected. You are the adult and have to teach your teenager how to become an adult by example.
- Communication is more about listening than it is about speaking. Learn how to listen empathically and how to speak assertively.
- You cannot win in an argument situation. Even if you win the argument, you lose the relationship. Always go for agreement. The way to do this is to have the mindset that everybody can win. It's called a Win-Win situation. You need to train your teenager to see that this is possible.
- Think about your emotional bank account and make frequent deposits of love and understanding.

Action Exercises

■ Make it your policy to avoid conflict. Be aware of situations where conflict can arise and guide yourself and your teenager away from these situations.

■ Learn about ego states and how to control your own. Learn how to control your temper. You want to spend all your time in ADULT or HAPPY PARENT. This will cause your teenager to spend time in ADULT or HAPPY CHILD.

■ Listen more than you speak. When you listen, make a big effort to understand where your teenager is, and put yourself there.

■ Make it family policy to go for Win-Win. Understand the ideas and teach them to the whole family. This is making a commitment to the happiness of your family.

■ Offer your teenager help with tasks or commitments that you think might be challenging. Even if the offer is refused, give reassurance that you are there and willing to help out should it be needed.

■ Teach the ideas of emotional bank accounts. Make it family policy to make regular deposits.

FOUR

When Communication Gets Difficult

Start with the end in mind

'**B**ut you just don't know my daughter,' said Tom in an exasperated voice.

'Yes, I do,' I replied. 'She's sometimes moody and silent. Occasionally she tries to bully you and she throws temper tantrums from time to time. There are times when she won't speak to you and looks at you almost with contempt. She sometimes gets locked in to destructive behaviours and just can't get out of them. When she feels frustrated, she takes it out on the nearest person.'

'How did you know that?' he asked.

'Simply because she's a teenager and teenagers are just like the rest of us,' I told him. 'What I've just done is describe every person you know. If you look carefully enough, you'll even see yourself in that description.'

There is a small number of typical difficult kinds of behaviour and we all use them to a greater or lesser extent at some time or other. Some youngsters are difficult nearly all of the time and all youngsters are difficult some of the time. The skill of dealing with difficult behaviour constructively lies in first of all recognizing and naming the behaviour, and then knowing how to defuse it. Once you've got out of the difficult behaviour you can start to get to a more positive behaviour.

Difficult behaviour always comes from the lack of a positive alternative. People always do what they think is best in any given situation. If positive and constructive behaviour patterns aren't available, then negative and destructive patterns are the obvious choice. Teenagers, by their nature, usually don't have the positive patterns – they haven't learned them yet. Because they don't have the positive patterns, and they so often see negative patterns being effective, that's what they use.

Difficult behaviour is hard to deal with precisely because we so often just get drawn into it. It's a caveman reaction, but it's much more common than most of us care to admit. When faced with an angry teenager, it's easy to get angry in return. When faced with an uncooperative teenager, it's all too easy to try to get your way by bullying and dominating. When faced with constant whingeing, it's easy to give in and agree to anything in order to stop the constant barrage of negativity and complaining. This is not constructive and is not going to improve the situation. If anything, it simply guarantees that difficult behaviour continues or even grows.

You already know that your teenager's mood and behaviour can affect you. What you need to become aware of is just how your behaviour can affect your teenager. You mustn't allow your teenager to dominate you and switch you from being a happy parent into an angry one. Rather you need to call on all your adult knowledge and experience to take control of difficult situations. This means staying on an even keel and keeping your temper under control.

The skill of handling any type of difficult behaviour falls into three fairly simple steps.

Firstly, you have to be able to identify the particular type of behaviour you're dealing with. The major types are described below. Study them carefully and see how they describe the types of behaviour that you see in your teenager. The descriptions may not be exact for your particular teenager, but they will probably be a fairly close fit. You may need to modify them a little to get an exact description.

Secondly, you then need to be able to gently and non-aggressively get the person out of the negative behaviour and lead them to a more positive and resourceful state. This involves a special kind of listening and responding. You need to listen hard and make the kind of responses that are going to affirm your teenager's right to his or her feelings. It is impossible to stay in a difficult behaviour state with someone who is affirming your rights! Your teenager has to become aware that agreement can only be reached when you are both in a state where you can go for a Win-Win situation. Highly negative behaviour isn't going to lead to it.

Finally, you need to solve the problem that caused the difficult behaviour in the first place, or at least help them to find their own solutions. Remember that it may not be possible to solve every problem. Sometimes you just have to accept that outside problems exist, and you have to learn to accept them and live with them. An example of this might be when your teenager is furious about being told to be home at a particular time. The solution to this is that your teenager simply has to accept that limits exist and that you can both agree what the limits are. These limits have to be set when you are both in a resourceful and positive state.

There are certainly going to be times when all this is not easy for you. Teenagers can be incredibly difficult at times and seem unlovable. These are the times that they need your love the most.

Chieftain Tank Charlie

A tank is a very effective attack weapon, and so is Charlie. He's abrupt, abusive and contemptuous. If his intimidation isn't enough then he'll use the big gun and blast you out of the way. His aim is to get you on the defensive and then overpower you. If that doesn't work, then he'll overwhelm you. The attack may be quite subtle at first, but if that isn't effective then it will become crude. The only important thing to Charlie is that he wins at all costs.

Charlie has got a strong need to prove that he's strong and always right. That means that you must be proven to be weak, always wrong, and not deserving of respect or mercy. Charlie thinks that the only person worthy of respect is himself and that a decisive victory is the way to get it. Mercy is only for the weak and Charlie is anything but weak.

Chieftain Tank Charlie has got three basic weapons in his armoury. He can roll over you and leave you crushed under his tracks. He's got high-powered machine guns to pin you down with rapid fire and he's got one big cannon to just blast you out of the way. Any of these weapons can be used at any time. The only result that Charlie is interested in is a devastating victory.

What to do

The one thing that you absolutely must avoid doing with Charlie is counter-attacking. Charlie isn't going to take any prisoners and he isn't going to be taken prisoner. His motto is almost certainly 'Death before dishonour' and loss of any battle is dishonour.

Your survival depends on a two-pronged defence. First of all, you have to have the strength to resist the attack and then allow him simply to run out of fuel. Don't do anything or say anything that is going to add fuel to his fire. Remain calm and only give answers that are neutral and meaningless – it's called artful vagueness.

Once the attack has run its course and Charlie has calmed down you can start to get to some kind of resolution. If you need to ask questions, make sure that they need thoughtful answers. The reason for this is that no one can think when they are angry and no one can be very angry while they are thinking deeply. As long as you lead Charlie towards rational thought, you are preventing another attack from being launched.

Make sure that you do address the causes of the attack and remember to aim for a Win-Win situation. Charlie needs to learn that he cannot bully you into submission and get away with it. You also need to understand that you can't do it to Charlie.

Landmine Luke

Step on the trigger and you're likely to lose a leg at the least. More likely, you're dead meat. Luke explodes without any apparent warning in a spectacular display of temper. He yells at you, loses control of what he says, stomps around, slams doors and throws things around, and can be a fearful sight. He is always verbally violent and can get physically violent as well. His physical violence may be slamming his fist on the table or even against a door or wall. In its worst case, it may be a direct physical attack on another person.

There are three things that set off Luke's trigger. These are frustration, threat and direct attack. When he feels frustrated that things aren't going the way that he wants them to go the pressure builds up inside him. At a certain point, he'll explode. When he feels frustrated or under threat, he may well go off without warning. And under direct attack his best defence is a devastating explosion to stop the attacker dead.

What to do

As with Charlie, you need to let the explosion happen and not respond. It will usually run its course without any help from you. Explosions caused by pent-up frustration are the most dangerous type. If Luke isn't calmed down, the explosion can cause a fire which feeds on itself and can get out of control. The way to calm him down is to agree that he has got a point.

Phrases such as 'Yes, Luke. I understand that you are upset about things', are the ones to go for. And use all your empathic listening skills.

If it goes on for too long and Luke seems to be working himself up into a fury, stop listening. Tantrums are only effective if there is an audience. Tell him quietly that you will not tolerate this kind of behaviour and that it must stop. Tell him that you both need time out to calm down and then leave.

Once Luke has calmed down you can discuss things normally and in an adult way, again going for a Win-Win solution.

Complaining Karen

When something goes wrong, as so often happens in life, Karen can always find out whose fault it is. She is an expert at laying the blame squarely on anyone except herself. Her speciality is finding problems and she does so with mono-tonous regularity. She not only finds the problems, she also knows that the solutions lie in someone else's hands. She always knows what other people should and shouldn't do. If only they did or didn't do these things, Karen's life would be much happier.

Frequently the blame lies with other people, but it might also be with society or the system in general. Everybody else is seen as being mean or selfish, or just plain uncaring and inconsiderate of other people's feelings and welfare. Although Karen can see that there are problems, she usually can't say exactly what they are. All she can see is that the glass is half-empty. Karen feels powerless to change things and can never see that she could have any part in making changes.

What to do

Karen loves having an audience, so be one. Listen attentively and lovingly. You may agree or disagree with what she has to say, but you need to remain neutral. Tell her that you understand her complaints, and gently point out that complaining never solved anything.

Guide Karen to an understanding that neither you nor she can solve other people's problems. If other people or outside situations are a problem for Karen, it is up to Karen to change her ideas about them.

Karen needs to know that it is pointless to complain about the injustices in the world, the poverty in Africa and infant mortality in India, and then simply to lay blame at everyone's doorstep. Now, if she worked hard and collected money, organized activities or started her own newsletter: that's a different matter.

This variation of Pastor Reinhold Niebuhr's Serenity Prayer is a useful one to use here.

> May I grow to have the serenity to accept the things I cannot change, the courage to change the things I can change and the wisdom to know the difference.

The solution to all Karen's problems lies in those simple words.

Silent Sally

It doesn't matter what you say to Sally, the reply is either silence, a mumbled reply or a simple 'yes' or 'no'. If you ask her if she had a nice day the reply will rarely be more than 'yes' or 'no', but you might be lucky and get a noncommittal, 'It was OK, I suppose'. If you ask for details, you won't get much in the way of clarification. If you ask what she did in school today the answer will be, 'Nothing much', or something similar. When you probe more deeply you'll likely get, 'Oh, get off my back, will you?' or 'It's not important', as a reply.

Sally avoids eye contact and looks sad and ill-at-ease for much of the time. She avoids opening up and will hardly ever show much enthusiasm for anything. She prefers to keep her opinions very much to herself.

Her silence can stem from any of several causes. It might be fear that you will be angry with her or belittle her for what she has to say and she's found that not saying much avoids this. She may be punishing you for something that you have done or said in the past which hurt her deeply. Silence can also come from spite. She thinks that if you are being mean to her, then she'll be mean to you in return. It might be because of a deep sadness in her and she's convinced that no one else could ever understand so there's not much point in speaking.

What to do

The one thing that you absolutely must avoid is yelling at her, 'Well if you won't speak to me, how can I help you?' If she'd really wanted your help, she would have asked for it. That she hasn't asked means that she doesn't want it or she thinks that she won't get it. There is a temptation to provoke an answer, even an angry one, but you must avoid this.

The best way into Sally's silent world is by patience. Lovingly and patiently asking about her life and the things that interest her will eventually get under her wall of silence. You might even try saying something completely wrong! 'David Beckham plays for Accrington Stanley, doesn't he?' might just get her to open up and put you right.

It may take some time, but you have to allow for this. Sally is still a little girl inside and wants your love. It's just that she doesn't know how to get it out of you.

Ask Sally open-ended questions. Those are the questions that begin with the question words who, what, where, when, why and how. Don't fill the silences with idle and nervous chatter of your own. Sally's eyes will just roll to the heavens and confirm to her that you're really not interested. Rather you should wait and maybe ask another question.

You can use the Friendly Silent Stare technique. You are thinking and projecting the thoughts that you really want to talk to your lovely Sally and it's making you sad that she won't take you on. Tell her in your mind how much you love her and want her to open up to you and the signals might just get there.

When Sally does open up, go easy on her. Don't imagine that you have conquered Everest. You probably haven't, but you've made it to the foothills. Gradually and slowly, build up your relationship and put as much love and laughter into her life as you can.

Know-It-All Nellie

There is no happier state than having the infinite wisdom of youth. When you know everything, you can put everyone else right and educate them. Your only reason for listening to anyone else is to know how wrong they are so you can then put them right on a few things.

Nellie is an expert on everything from fox-hunting to international affairs and her opinion is worth much more than anyone's factual knowledge. She sees everything in black and white and knows that if you aren't in perfect agreement with her, then you are wrong. She has an unshakable belief in her own superiority and rightness in everything. She'll bulldoze her way through any contrary knowledge or opinions with put downs, ridicule and even anger that you could be so stupid.

Nellie just loves thinking. She spends hours reconfirming her own superiority and congratulating herself on her own brilliance. She probably has a small group of friends who are almost identical in every thought. They form her intellectual support system and together they put the world to rights.

What to do

Nellie just loves arguing, so let her. But remember that you can't win an argument. Even if you win the argument, you lose the relationship, especially with Nellie. You don't need to win the argument: you need to help Nellie argue herself into good, flexible thinking.

Ask Nellie for her opinions on everything and let her go. Don't argue your point; just give Nellie the chance to really sort out her thinking for herself. You can then encourage her to get the facts right by going on the Internet or checking out books from the library. Encourage her to see the same argument from the opposite point of view. If she's a vegetarian, for example, ask her to put the argument from the point of view of a southern Sudanese tribesman for whom cattle equals wealth.

If she wants to argue about house rules, invite her to swap roles with you. Allow her to set the rules given certain agreed facts about parents and children. She will probably come up with a set of rules that are more restrictive than any that you, with your adult perspective, would ever dream of.

What's-The-Point Willie

There is no point in doing anything as far as Willie is concerned. He'll tell you that the government is manufacturing super-lethal genetically engineered Ebola viruses and we'll all be dead in fifteen years when they escape. In Willie's view, education is pointless. Only yesterday, he read about a person with a PhD who hasn't had a job for years. Books are boring. Going out is boring. Staying in is boring. Sports are boring. In fact, there isn't anything much that isn't boring.

Willie is cynical about everything. About the only things he can get enthusiastic about are conspiracy theories and negativity. He hasn't got much respect for anybody and can describe them all as nerds, dorks, jerks, boffins or just plain boring. He knows that you can't fight the system so there isn't really much point in trying. If you ask him is the glass half-full or half-empty, he'll reply, 'Who cares?'

> Father: 'What's the problem, son? Is it ignorance or apathy?'
> Son: 'I don't know and I don't care.'

What to do

You have to realize that all Willie's ideas are based on negative thinking. It's not that he doesn't think, he probably spends ages in his room thinking doom and gloom and finds plenty of evidence to convince him that he is right. Your main hope of breaking this cycle lies in a simple sentence. 'You might be right, but what if you are wrong?'

There is plenty of evidence to show Willie that he is right, and there is much more to show that he is wrong. All he really needs to do is to find it. Governments have been conducting experiments with toxins for many years, but we are all still alive. There are a few people with PhDs who haven't got jobs, and there are thousands more who have got excellent jobs and some are millionaires.

Negative thinking can never be argued away; it can only be replaced by positive thinking.

Warning: If Willie really cannot get out of negative thinking, he may be on his way into depression. This needs to be taken seriously. It needs to be diagnosed by a professional and therapy prescribed.

Sniper Sam

Sam doesn't like to face the enemy. His way of getting the kill is to lie in wait and take shots from a safe distance or from a place of easy escape. Sometimes he'll lie in wait for days to get a good shot, but he's ready to take a shot whenever the opportunity arises. His weapon is a small-bore rifle firing poisoned darts. The killing ability relies on accuracy and timing.

What to do

You have to take Sam on and not allow him to get away with nasty, snide shots from a distance. You must not allow yourself to be wound up, or Sam has scored a kill. Rather, you must have the strength of resolve to dodge all the darts or simply allow them to bounce off harmlessly.

Don't allow Sam to escape. Tackle him head on and assertively point out that you will not tolerate nastiness and snide comments. Tell him that adults don't do that, and you don't need to see or hear that again. Sam will often try to laugh it off and tell you he was only joking. Again, be assertive and point out that it's only funny if everyone thinks it's funny. You don't. You think it's nasty and below the standards you'd expect.

Dealing with put downs

If there is one thing that most teenagers are experts at, it's the put down. This is the word or phrase that either ends a conversation by cutting you dead and leaving you angry and frustrated, or drives you into a blind fury. They are common devices that teenagers use between themselves and they are offensive.

Put downs are a substitute for good thinking and they are inevitably used when there is a sense that the discussion is not going the way your teenager wants. What happens is that your teenager can see the weakness in his or her own argument and doesn't like the inevitable result. The best way to prevent the outcome is to stop the discussion going any further. Hence the put down.

One of the problems that teenagers cannot see is that, to an adult, these put downs are like a red rag to a bull. You mustn't allow yourself to be thrown off course by them. They are only effective if they cause you to lose control of the conversation. This means that you either lose your temper or simply refuse to continue. If you maintain a calm, cool exterior and allow the put down to bounce off you harmlessly, you completely neutralize its effect. You need to arm yourself with strategies to deal with any put downs that come your way and make sure that they simply do not work.

Some of the more common put downs are:

Put down	Possible reply
I don't think so.	OK. What do you think? It may well be that I have misunderstood the situation and I'd like to understand it correctly. I really want your help with this one.
Whatever!	Oh, so whatever I decide is acceptable to you, is it? I'd much prefer that we decide together. If you leave it up to me, my decision is . . . Is that acceptable to you or do you want to discuss it some more?
That's sad.	I'm sorry, but I don't understand what you think is sad. I'd always thought that doing the right thing was the right thing to do. Why is that not so?
Get real.	In what way is what I'm saying not realistic? I understand that we have different views, and I need you to help me see reality from your point of view.
That stinks.	Oh? I'm sorry. I've tried to be polite and constructive. What is it exactly that you find offensive about what I've said?
Even you . . .	It sounds like you think I'm of limited intelligence. Why, exactly, do you think that?
As if.	It sounds like you think that is unrealistic. Why exactly is that?
Are you going to make me?	No, I can't make you do the right thing. Only you can do that. All I'm asking is that you face up to your responsibilities. That's what adults do all the time.
Perfect! (Said in a sarcastic tone.)	Really? What you say and the way you're saying it confuses me.

You can easily build up your own list of put downs and possible replies.

Your major defence when faced with any type of aggressive talk is that you must take the words at face value. Completely ignore any venom behind them. This reduces their impact on you and challenges your teenager to do some proper thinking. It's only by both of you doing this proper thinking that you can hope to make any real progress and get to civilized adult-to-adult conversation.

In the case of sarcasm, the approach is different. You have to point out unemotionally that the words and the tone of voice don't match up. Then you question which meaning is intended. Is it the words or the tone of voice? If it is the words, that's OK. If it is the tone of voice, then more intelligent and adult-to-adult conversation is needed.

Review

Some people are difficult nearly all the time. All people are difficult some of the time. There is only a small number of ways of being difficult. All difficult behaviour can be overcome and turned around if you use the right techniques at the right time and in the right way.

Action Exercises

■ Observe your teenager carefully and analyse difficult behaviour. Choose your responses carefully. Always defuse difficult situations and take control for yourself. Teach your teenager that difficult behaviour will *never* get good results.

FIVE

Communicating With School

Start with the end in mind

Schools have changed in the past twenty or so years and they continue to change. In the past, they saw themselves as places where children came to be educated. These days they see themselves more as places where children come to learn. The difference is more than just one of words; it is quite astounding. In the past, parents were seen mainly as a problem to be solved and as something to be avoided except in the case of trouble. Today parents are seen as having a positive contribution to make towards their children's education. This is, of course, much more in keeping with reality.

These days you are likely to get a letter telling you what wonderful work your child has been doing and how good they have been. In the past, you would only get a letter if there was a problem. This is a wonderful change and is only a small part of the whole. The basic reality is that schools are now much more child-centred than teacher-centred.

If you have any concerns or problems or need to communicate with school for any reason, you will find that the school will be happy to see you. Schools now have staff that are trained in every aspect of looking after children and helping them to develop in positive ways. No matter what you want to discuss, you'll find someone who is expert enough to deal with your concerns. The strong probability is that they will also know your teenager personally and be able to give personalized and customized help. Even if the kind of help or advice is not available from school, the LEA will have someone or access to someone who can help. Either you will be referred to them by the school or the school will communicate with them directly.

Preparing yourself

Before you make any contact with the school, you should make a note of everything that you feel needs to be talked about. This will include questions that you want to ask and information that you want to give. You must appreciate that schools are busy places and that teachers are busy people. They will certainly be more than willing and able to give you time, but will not appreciate having to go fishing for information.

When seeing anyone in a school, you are dealing with a highly trained professional. They will have most of the answers either in their heads or in a file somewhere which they can go to immediately. You must respect this and have all your questions prepared.

If there is any information that you have which will affect either your teenager's education or social and moral well-being, prepare it in advance. Don't be in the least bit concerned about giving sensitive information. School staff are highly professional and would never dream of allowing information of a personal nature to become common knowledge. They are bound by regulations and a strict code of conduct. Teachers do chat about pupils in the staffroom, but not in a nasty way and *never* about sensitive issues.

When you meet with a teacher or other professional in school, you are dealing with another human being. I know that teachers aren't often seen as such, but take it from me, they all are. They have exactly the same hopes, wants and desires as the rest of us. Amongst other things, they like to be treated with as much respect as anyone else. No one, especially a teacher, likes to have the law laid down in front of them and to be told what is what. When you are well prepared, you are much more likely to have a positive discussion and get much more help.

Parent-teacher consultations

These consultations may be held anywhere from once a year to once a term. Some schools open the school for an entire day for all pupils and their parents. Others open for a few hours in the evenings for a single year group at a time. You will have the opportunity to meet all the teachers that your teenager sees and to discuss your child's progress. I cannot stress strongly enough the benefit that these consultations have for all concerned.

The teacher will probably show you your teenager's notebook and make useful comments on progress and general behaviour. Teachers are urged to accentuate the positive, but will also mention any special worries that they may have. Even though you will only get a few minutes with each of the teachers, you can get a strong sense both of how your teenager is making progress and how the school is helping your teenager. If you have any particular points that you need to raise, this is the best time to do it.

This is also a good time to mention anything that you think might be useful. In my time, I have picked up some important information about youngsters from chance remarks dropped by parents. This can vary from favourite sports and hobbies to family relationships with other youngsters that I had no idea about. Information is power to a teacher's understanding and interactions with youngsters.

Almost without fail, the last question that a parent asks just before going is, 'What can I do to help?' I, for one, could never answer that question well. I don't know many teachers who can in the time available. That's why I've spent five months researching and writing this book!

For general points

The first point of contact for most things will be your teenager's form tutor. He or she will see your teenager twice a day and will have a close personal knowledge of them. The form tutor is responsible for things like checking attendance and collecting absence notes, making sure that homework diaries are kept up to date and that homework is done regularly, and that the youngsters are generally happy and getting on well. Other tasks include things like collecting merit marks and issuing merit certificates, delivering detention notes from other teachers and so forth. Tutors try to spend a little time with group members and really get to know the youngsters. This all goes to make sure that the tutor builds up an accurate picture of each of the group and can tell when things are going right and when they are going wrong.

For more weighty matters, you may want to see your teenager's head of year. These people are amongst the most highly trained and dedicated people you will ever meet in any profession anywhere. Their day is spent not only teaching (most will spend most of their time teaching), but also dealing with every aspect of children's school and outside lives. There are rarely things that need to be discussed that these wonderful people have not seen before. Heads of year are always experienced teachers and have had many years of dealing with all sorts of children from gifted and talented to those who have profound difficulties. They have also experienced some cooperative youngsters and some for whom conflict is a way of life.

The sort of things that heads of year deal with are many and varied, but tend to fall into just a few categories. Amongst these are: personal welfare; attendance; general academic performance; and behaviour issues. No matter what your concerns or observations, you can be confident that you will get the help that you need.

You might find that you are invited to come and see the head of year if there are any points they feel are important to discuss. Don't worry. If there are problems, even big problems, you will find that you get all the help and support you need. When problems do arise, the head of year will be looking for your help to get them resolved. They are wise enough to know that teenagers frequently cannot help themselves. They are also wise enough and experienced enough to know that a positive effort from you and them is usually enough to help most youngsters over even the stickiest of patches. If it isn't, you will find that professional help is brought in and that any remaining problems are usually solved this way.

In the case of consistent misbehaviour, all schools have what are called behaviour management plans. These are usually administered by heads of year. The plans give the youngsters specific behaviour goals to achieve and monitor progress towards these goals. The youngsters are put 'on report' and the reports are signed and filled in by each teacher on a lesson-by-lesson and day-by-day basis. If your teenager is put on report, you will be informed and kept posted as to the changes in behaviour that are needed. It can be quite distressing to have your teenager on report. Rest assured that the intention is purely to help your teenager adopt new and constructive behaviour patterns. There is no suggestion of punishment. Although, if the behaviour doesn't change, then punishments will very likely follow.

For subject-specific points

If you have any points to make about any aspect of your teenager's work in subject areas, go directly to the teacher concerned. If it is simply to give information, a simple and to-the-point explanation is quite sufficient. Teachers neither want nor need flowery notes explaining all about everything. It is quite sufficient to explain that a particular piece of homework wasn't done because of family commitments. The teacher doesn't need or want to know all about the event in its finest detail.

If the points are more complex or you have real worries, ask the teacher to phone you and arrange an appointment. It would be helpful if you could give the teacher a guide as to what times are good for you. Trying to telephone a teacher at school is a heartbreaking business. They are so busy and get so little free time that you are unlikely to be successful. Even if you did manage to get hold of the teacher, they would probably be doing ten other things at the same time. If you do need to make an urgent appointment, phone the school secretary and leave a message for the teacher to call you back. You can outline the details of your concern to help them help you better.

You may wish to have your teenager present or you may prefer to keep it private. It depends very much on what is being discussed. If your teenager is present, involve him or her in the discussion as much as possible. There is nothing more depressing to a teenager that to sit quietly while other people are talking about you. This is doubly true if the talk isn't very positive.

If you think that the discussion could get nasty (i.e. if there is personal animosity), you might also ask that a senior member of staff is present to moderate things. Teenagers often get the wrong end of the stick and can become quite upset if they feel that they are being got at.

Always go into such a conference with the attitude that an amicable and positive result is possible. You might find that a younger teacher has a rather fearful attitude to discussing things with a parent. If this is the case, you need to be able to take positive control for yourself and steer things towards a good outcome.

One of my youngsters is dyslexic. His homework is frequently rather scruffy and is not always completed. I sometimes write a little note to the teacher explaining things. I point out just how hard he has worked and that we are both proud of his efforts. I know that the teachers appreciate this and my son certainly does. If your teenager has similar problems, you might want to do the same.

Punishments

Schools are a reflection of society. When people offend against society, punishments are frequently applied. Exactly the same happens in school. Schools don't like doing this and, quite frankly, they know full well that punishments rarely work in the way intended. The problem is finding alternatives.

If your teenager is frequently kept in detention or has other forms of punishment applied, it is a sure sign that there are some significant problems. If punishments are frequently applied, it is a sure sign that they aren't working. As previously discussed, you don't make people do good by making them feel bad. The only result of a punishment is to make someone feel resentful and negative towards the punisher. When the punisher is a teacher or a school, there isn't going to be much enthusiasm about school or much learning going on there.

If this is the case for your teenager, you need to visit the school and find some alternative recompense that doesn't involve punishment. Remember that you want a win-win situation. Your teenager should win by overcoming negative behaviours and attitudes. The school should win by helping your teenager to behave more appropriately. And, of course, you will win by having a much happier and more motivated teenager.

I would suggest that any and every offence against school rules is dealt with by your teenager in writing.

Your teenager should write a note or letter containing three elements. The first is an admission of guilt and an explanation of why the offence occurred. The second part should be an understanding of why the offence occurred and an explanation of why it was the wrong choice to make. The final element should be a promise that the offence will not occur in future and what they will do to ensure that this promise is kept.

I cannot imagine any school refusing to allow this, at least as an experiment. I predict that the change in behaviour required is much more likely to occur using this approach.

Term-time holidays

Recently the UK government has introduced a new regulation concerning parents taking children out of school for holidays. The legislation provides for schools to issue fines in the case of unauthorized absences. I have yet to meet a head teacher who has anything other than concern about this. Heads never become heads in order to issue fines and punish people. The sole reason that they become heads is because they have the vision and the skills to create a wonderful learning environment for youngsters. They all realize that their job is to work with parents and children and not against them. None of them thinks that issuing fines to parents is going to create a positive and cooperative family–school partnership.

If your youngster were to get the opportunity to go trekking in the Himalayas or sailing down the Amazon, the head would almost certainly agree without any hesitation. If someone is going to Guatemala or some other exotic place on business and can take your teenager, that would also be agreed to. These experiences would expand any youngster's horizons, and that is largely what heads think their schools are about. They are wise enough to realize that the whole world is a school, not only their little part of it.

On the other hand, if the holiday is requested during school time simply because there's a 50 per cent discount, that's a different matter. Permission would likely be refused unless there was a strong case to be made. In this case, any absence would be recorded as unauthorized and the school or LEA could impose sanctions.

Of course, every case is going to have different pros and cons, and every head is an individual. I would strongly advise that you prepare a strong case for any term-time absences and present it to the head. But you must be aware that permission can be refused.

Review

- Schools these days recognize that they must have a partnership with parents and children if they are to be effective. The school may contact you to let you know about significant achievement or about problems.
- If you need to contact the school, your teenager's form tutor is usually the first point of contact. Heads of year normally deal with matters that are more serious.
- If your teenager is put on report, the intent is to help achieve acceptable behaviour. Only if this fails will punishments be applied. You can always suggest alternatives to punishments. The school will probably agree, at least as an experiment.

SIX

Establishing Rules

Start with the end in mind

As soon as my youngest son started school, he started learning from his school friends. Many of the things he learned were things I didn't like much. The first thing was that he learned how to jump on furniture – a big no-no in my house and on my furniture. This had to stop, so a rule was introduced. He next learned to run in the house. Another no-no, so another rule. And so it went on and on and on . . . Here was my son not yet even five years old, and I was expecting him to remember a set of rules that would have taxed the memory of a high-court judge.

I was creating an incredibly complex system. It went like this. Something goes against what I like. I create a rule. Something else happens. I create another rule. This continues until we have a set of rules. One of the rules gets broken. (He is, after all, just a little boy.) I get angry. I create another rule. Another rule gets broken. I get angrier still and create yet another rule.

The poor little lad couldn't possibly remember all these rules, and every rule broken was sending my blood pressure sky high. I was unknowingly creating a system that was perfectly designed to do two things. First of all, it was bound to fail to do what I wanted it to do because he was just a little boy. He couldn't be expected to remember all this stuff. I was setting him up for failure. Secondly, it was perfectly designed to allow me to find fault as the rules were inevitably going to be broken. I was setting myself up for failure.

Luckily for me, at about this time I was studying systems thinking. This is a fascinating topic that looks at the underlying simplicity of complex systems. The systems I was studying referred to learning, but it is relevant to any kind of system. I realized that my family was also a system of people living in a set of situations. One of the most important ideas of systems thinking is looking for leverage. This means asking what is the smallest change that can be made which will push the system in the direction that you want it to go. The answer is to make the system as simple as possible and make it 'people friendly'.

There are only two rules

It sometimes comes as a surprise to people when I say that there are only two rules, but it is perfectly true. Every rule, directive or law in a democratic society is based upon one or both of the basic rules. Even the Ten Commandments can easily be understood in these terms. These two rules are of such basic importance and of such a universal nature that it is impossible to overstate their importance. They are:

- respect; and
- health and safety first.

As long as these two things are in place, there's not much that can go wrong. There is no likelihood of anyone behaving inappropriately or getting hurt or upset.

Respect people, their feelings, property and culture

These are four important aspects to respect, each of which must be in place to fulfil the rule completely.

Respect for self

This means feeling good about yourself. It means knowing that you are doing the right things by yourself and knowing that the things that you do will impress others by their rightness. Respect for self means eating well and avoiding foods with chemical additives. It means getting the right amount of exercise and high-quality rest and sleep. It means leading a balanced life. It means having fun and being bright and positive about life and all that it has to offer. Working at the right time, relaxing at the right time, being quiet and being raucous at the right time are all important parts of life.

Respect for others

This means treating other people as they wish to be treated. It means speaking and behaving pleasantly. There is nothing to be gained and everything to be lost by behaving towards others in a disrespectful way. There are always going to be times of conflict, this is perfectly natural and is to be expected. But even being in conflict doesn't mean that respect cannot exist. You will unfailingly find that respectful behaviour will help you either to come to an agreement or to agree to disagree agreeably. This is difficult for teenagers. They generally feel that life is made up of winners and losers.

Respect for property

This means looking after your own and other people's property, maintaining it in good order and storing it tidily when it's not in use. It means not causing any damage or being untidy. If you own it, look after it. If you borrow, take good care of it and return it promptly. If you break it, fix it or replace it. If you lose it, find it or replace it. When you've finished with it, dispose of it properly.

Respect for culture

This means respecting your own family culture, local culture and national culture and, of course, that of other people. When your teenager respects family, local and national cultures, he becomes part of them, and develops feelings for other people. Respecting the cultures of other people means growing up to be free of prejudice. You can see how these are adult ways of thinking.

Health and safety

This means physical health and safety: ensuring that pain and physical injury do not happen. It also means emotional, spiritual and moral health and safety: making sure that no one is in danger of having their emotional, spiritual or moral well-being put in danger.

Health and safety of self

Everybody over a few years of age has the primary responsibility for their own health and safety. Parents and others cannot be expected always to be in attendance to give guidance and control. The simple statement is: if it isn't safe and healthy, don't do it. This applies to both physical and mental activities! Dangerous physical activities can, and frequently do, lead to avoidable injury. Dangerous thoughts lead to unhappiness and possibly depression, and can lead, in turn, to dangerous physical activities. Remember that this is a difficult one for teenagers – they really do believe that they are immortal and unique.

Health and safety of others

Apart from the obvious need never to place others in the path of danger, it also means being supportive and giving wise help and advice as well as physical assistance at times. This means that there is a need to look out for the safety of other people and to take on the role of protector. If you know of someone who is putting themselves in danger, you do have a moral obligation to help them avoid it.

The universal nature of these rules

These are the only rules that your family needs. You will find that every justifiable law and rule, written or unwritten, has been put in place to ensure that either respect or safety, or both, is maintained. This is a fruitful topic for family discussion and I recommend this to you.

What does and doesn't work

We learn to do things by doing them. As long as they work, we continue doing them and we expect to keep on getting the same results. When our children are small we have to tell them what to do for much of the time and they do what they are told. Hey! We've found a system that works.

Then our children grow and develop and we try using the same things that have worked in the past. Because your child is now a teenager and growing towards independence, your systems don't work as well as they did. So what do you do? You do the obvious thing. You do the same thing, but more of it. It still doesn't work. So you do more and more and more of the same thing and it still doesn't work. You're creating more problems and solving none of them.

> If you're getting deeper and deeper into a hole, stop digging!

Your teenager is changing so the things you do have to be adapted to suit this new person. You need to re-assess the things that you do and the way in which you do them. Find what doesn't work and stop doing it and replace it with what does work.

What doesn't work

Telling doesn't work. You can tell your teenagers from now until eternity, and it won't make a blind bit of difference. Teenagers (in their opinion) know everything and you, as an adult (again, in their opinion), know nothing of value, so why should they listen? Do you like being told what to do?

Lecturing doesn't work. It's even worse than telling. Lectures are always understood as being criticism, and no one likes that! You probably remember teachers at school who used this technique. How did you feel about them? Well, that's the same way your teenager feels when you do it. Do you like being lectured?

Yelling is even worse than telling. The lesson you are teaching is that out-of-control behaviour is quite acceptable to get what you want. Now it might be that what you want is quite reasonable and you might be quite justified in being angry that you don't get it. Nevertheless, yelling isn't productive. It might get you what you want this time, but you will probably have to yell even louder next time. How do you feel about people who yell at you?

Nagging doesn't work. How many nagging people do you know who claim any form of success for their nagging? The one thing that nagging will ensure is that the nagger is never listened to. Nagging is ineffective. Worse, it is destructive. It's destructive to the desired purpose and it's destructive to love. Face it – no one can find it easy to love someone who nags incessantly. If they do, it's a testimony to the power of love and not the power of nagging. Do you like being nagged and nagged and nagged and . . . ?

Bribing doesn't work. The obvious problem with bribing is that the size and cost of the bribe increases with the age of the child. The promise of a lollipop might bribe a two-year-old to stop screaming, but try that with a stroppy sixteen-year-old. Nothing less than a new stereo system will work!

Marvin Marshall makes the excellent point that bribes for expected behaviour are quite simply contrary to what happens in reality. 'When,' he asks, 'was the last time you were rewarded for stopping at a red light?' Exceptionally good behaviour or achievement can certainly be recognized and celebrated, perhaps with a gift or a special treat, but expected behaviour is expected without bribes.

Pleading doesn't work. Begging your teenager to have respect for the house and to behave nicely when Auntie Agnes comes to visit is demeaning. When you beg, you are saying goodbye to your authority. You must never help your teenager to think that behaving well is a favour.

Punishing doesn't work. Can you imagine your teenager saying, 'Thanks for the clip round the ear, Dad. That really helps me'? No, you can't, and it will never happen. Who do you know who is happy about having to pay a parking fine?

All of the things above only ever serve to produce bad feelings and resentment. And bad feelings don't produce good behaviour. All the above techniques have three things in common which virtually guarantee failure to produce good results.

- Firstly, answer this question: who is doing and who is being done to? The answer is, of course, that you are doing the work and you are doing the thinking. Your teenager is on the receiving end of a tongue-lashing and is quite passive. There is no need for him to do anything other than roll his eyes up to heaven! You are also, of course, stressing yourself out as well as your teenager.

- The second point is that all these things make your teenager feel bad, and no one does good when they feel bad! If you want your teenager to do good, then make him feel good! In order to do good things, one needs to be in a resourceful mental state, and no one gets into a resourceful state when being nagged or lectured, yelled at or otherwise made to feel small and resentful.

- The third thing is that they are all dependent on supervision. What happens when no one is supervising? What is in place that is going to ensure that rule-following becomes a natural part of your teenager's life? They all remove the responsibility for good behaviour from your teenager's shoulders (where it belongs) onto your shoulders (where it doesn't belong).

In using any of these techniques in the quest to raise your teenagers to obey the rules, you have set yourself up for failure! If failure doesn't follow, it says more about your teenagers than it does about these techniques.

What does work

Respecting the feelings of your teenager is vital. Teenagers are going through an emotional time that is quite difficult enough. Your job as a parent is to help them get through the time with emotions and self-image in good condition. How do you like to be spoken to? Speak to your teenager in the same way. How does your teenager want to be spoken to? Ask and find out. Then make sure that you use the information.

Asking for what you want using 'I' language. Even the stroppiest of teenagers is still a child at heart, and children have a built-in desire to please their parents. If you make it pleasantly clear what you want, your teenager is almost forced by nature to comply. 'I really would like it if you hung your coat up immediately you came in the house,' said pleasantly is likely to get a good response. Yelling 'Will you pick up that coat and hang it up, please?' isn't going to get much joyful cooperation.

Encouraging and appreciating success is always better than criticizing failure. Your teenager really does have a lot of good qualities. It might be a good sense of humour; it might be faithfulness to friends or maybe some special gift like drawing or a good singing voice. Get into the habit of finding things that you can say positive things about. When you affirm these things, your teenager gets a buzz from it. Everybody craves admiration and appreciation. Be the one to give it in bucketfulls.

Saying 'yes' whenever possible is always going to be better than saying 'no' automatically. Your teenager is looking for your permission to grow up. Grant it and, if you like, make it dependent on something else. 'No, you can't go out until you've finished your homework' and 'Yes, you can go out as soon as you've finished your homework' mean exactly the same. But which one would your teenager rather hear? Which one would you rather say?

Correcting poor behaviour or attitudes with a simple question: Is this going to get you/us what you/we want? Your job is to get your teenager to get focused on positive and helpful behaviours and away from the alternatives. Teenagers don't always know what they want and they often do the things which are only going to get them grief. This simple question can make all the difference in creating the right mindset.

Asking 'What are the two rules?' This immediately shows that one or other, or maybe both of the rules, are being broken. Your teenager needs to stop and think about things in basic and fundamental ways. Simply by doing this, your teenager is preparing to develop into the post-conventional stage of maturity. And that, if you remember, means becoming more and more adult.

You can't break the rules

There is a common idea that rules are there to be broken. I've got a lot of sympathy with that view and, if the truth were known, break a lot of them myself. But it is only true in the case of silly and trivial rules put in place by silly authorities. I'm not talking about these petty rules here; I'm talking about the two rules of respect and safety. These rules are absolutely unbreakable simply because they are so universal. It's because they are universal that I suggest they are the only two rules you need.

The full statement of this principle is:

> You cannot break the rules. You can only break yourself against the rules.

This principle is not too difficult to understand. If you try to break the rule of respect, you will finish up not being respected or trusted. In order to gain respect, you have to give respect. In order to be trusted, you have to be trustworthy. The lack of respect and trust affects the individual concerned, not society in general. It is the individual who is broken. This is, of course, just as true for government, police, teachers and parents and all other people and institutions as it is for teenagers.

If the rule of safety is broken, damage to people or property will inevitably follow. The individual or property that suffered is damaged or broken in some way. The reputation of the individual who caused the damage is similarly damaged or broken.

In any case, the rules are never broken. Only the people who attempt to break them.

Review

- Positive and constructive language is *always* better than negative and destructive language.
- There are only two rules: (i) respect; and (ii) health and safety.
- You cannot break the rules. You can only break yourself against the rules.

Action Exercises

■ Learn and teach the two rules. Use them as an everyday part of your language.

■ Listen to yourself. Do you always model the types of behaviour that you want your teenager to use? Always speak and behave respectfully and teach your teenager to do the same.

■ Look for opportunities to say nice things and grab them as they come. Make it a habit to focus on positive things.

SEVEN

Responsibility and Self-Discipline

Start with the end in mind

Dr Stephen Covey defines responsibility very nicely. He defines it as being the **ability** to choose the right **response**. This flies in the face of common wisdom. The common wisdom is that my behaviour towards a person or situation depends on that person's behaviour towards me or the situation. This doesn't have to be the case. I can choose how I respond. I can be reactive or proactive.

Reactive behaviour is when I allow people or situations to control me. I react according to well-known patterns. If a person is good toward me, I am good toward them. If a situation is to my liking, I am happy. If a situation is not to my liking, I am unhappy. A few moments' thought will convince you that this is really immature and irresponsible. I am ceding control of myself to other people.

Proactive behaviour is when I choose my response to people and situations. I pro-act according to how I feel the best outcomes will happen. I can choose to be happy or unhappy. I can choose to be calm and collected or to lose my temper. Being proactive is being mature and responsible: being able to choose your own response to any given situation.

When your teenager was a baby, she cried when she was hungry. As she grew bigger and more able to look after herself, she learned how to ask. As she grew bigger still, she learned how to go into the kitchen and make herself a sandwich. Hopefully, later still, she learned to make the sandwich and then clear up after herself leaving the kitchen clean and tidy. This is a natural growth, and it needs to continue past the childhood years into the teenage years and beyond.

Adults are often unfair to youngsters. All too often we yell at teenagers or punish them for making the wrong decision when we haven't let them know what the right decisions are or taught how to make them independently. In order to make the right choices, teenagers need to know what their options are. Teenagers need to learn they *always* have a choice, and the choices they make determine their maturity.

The ultimate test of responsibility is how your teenager behaves when no one is there to supervise. We all have times when we are challenged. It may be finding a wallet in the street when no one else is around. It may be resisting peer pressure to behave badly or even get into crime. It's a moment of choice. Responsibility is neither more nor less than choosing the right course of action in this moment. It is choosing what is right simply because it is right.

The four quadrants of behaviour

Behaviour can always be classified in two different ways. The two ways are:

- behaviour is either respectful and safe or disrespectful and/or unsafe; and
- behaviour is either conscious or unconscious.

Using this simple way of looking at behaviour we can define a set of quadrants. All behaviour will fall into one of the four quadrants. There is therefore a simple and easily understood way of describing behaviour.

The four quadrants

The quadrants separate these two important ideas. They do this by considering any behaviour as being made up of both quality and consciousness. The top row indicates that behaviour is acceptable in that due respect is shown and the safety of all is assured. The bottom row indicates behaviour in which respect and/or safety is compromised. The right-hand column is for behaviour that doesn't require conscious thought. The left-hand column shows that the behaviour is deliberate.

	Conscious	**Unconscious**	**Result**
Respect and safety	C = Cooperation Complies with requests	D = Democracy Complies with standards unconsciously	Everybody wins
No respect or safety	B = Bothering Deliberate non-compliance	A = Anarchy Out-of-control behaviour	Everybody loses

You can see immediately how powerful the system is. Behaviour is identified precisely as being acceptable or unacceptable. It is also identified as being with or without conscious effort.

The next table is a more comprehensive description of standards of behaviour.

	Conscious	**Unconscious**	**Result**
Respect and safety = H (high)	**Cooperation** Proceed with caution. ■ Standards are recognized and adhered to under supervision. Requests are complied with immediately and willingly. Limited confidence in individual. ■ Cooperation requires no responsibility. ■ Motivation is external.	**Democracy** Go forward with confidence. ■ Adult behaviour. The standards are a part of nature and obeyed without thought. There is no need for supervision. Confidence in and respect for individual. ■ Democracy requires full responsibility. ■ Motivation is internal.	Every-body wins.
No respect or safety = L (low)	**Bothering** This must stop immediately. ■ Standards are recognized, but not adhered to. Wilful disobedience. Requests have to be repeated before being complied with or are complied with unwillingly, often with disrespectful body language, back-chat or impertinence. ■ In need of corrective action. ■ Motivation is selfishness.	**Anarchy** This must stop immediately. ■ No standards are recognized. Behaviour is out of control. Extreme selfishness. Requests are not complied with. Impolite or offensive language used. Possible threats of violence or actual violence used. Real danger of damage to persons and property. ■ In need of immediate prevention. ■ Motivation is non-existent.	Every-body loses.

The four quadrants of behaviour system

You can also identify the *level* of behaviour:

- H is acceptable = high-level behaviour (= C or D).
- L is unacceptable = low-level behaviour (= A or B).

This is a useful and quick shorthand to use.

How to use the four quadrants

The system is incredibly simple and easy to understand. This is because the two distinct ideas of acceptable and unacceptable are quite simple and so are the ideas of with and without deliberate thought. Therefore, there can be absolutely no doubt about what quadrant any particular behaviour is in.

A fundamental idea is to separate the person from the deed. This means that you are putting a label on the behaviour which is unacceptable, not labelling the person. We want to talk about good or bad behaviour not good or bad people. Although people are frequently known by what they do, it is not always the most helpful way to describe them.

Stage 1 – teach the quadrants

You have to spend some time sitting down looking at the quadrants together, and discussing them and what they mean. Talk about different family, social and school situations and what behaviour in each quadrant would be like. As a simple example, take tidiness:

A	Permanent mess making. Takes something out of a drawer and just leaves it where it's finished with. Throws things in drawers at random. No consideration for other people or their property. Will not clean up even when asked. Feels no responsibility for family standards.
B	Deliberately makes a mess. Will intentionally leave things lying around just to cause problems. When asked to help clear up, makes a big fuss. Has to be asked more than once. Needs to be kept on task. Frequently complains about having to help around the house.
C	Usually tidy, but sometimes makes a mess. Will clear up cheerfully when asked.
D	Clears up after self and helps others. Feels responsibility to create a nice clean and tidy house for everyone to live in.

You can easily create lots of situations that you might want to discuss. Some examples might be:

- family relationships;
- at-school behaviour;
- homework;
- playing music; and
- in-the-street behaviour.

In each case, discuss the typical types of behaviour that would fit into each of the quadrants. It is vitally important that everyone in the family is strongly aware of exactly what the different standards mean and how they are constructed. It is important that everybody speaks the same language and understands exactly what is being said by everyone else.

Stage 2 – Define adulthood

Your teenager wants to be treated like an adult, but doesn't know what adult behaviour is. You need to discuss together exactly how real adults behave – and it's so simple. Real adults' behaviour is in quadrants D and C. As soon as behaviour slips into quadrants A or B, that is a sure sign of immaturity.

If your teenager ever asks you, 'When are you going to start treating me like an adult?' you have the perfect answer. You simply reply, 'When am I going to know that you are an adult?'

The only possible answer to this is, 'When my behaviour is consistently in quadrants C and D.' Since the question only ever comes when teenagers are behaving in A or B, their own answer changes the behaviour. There are no arguments. There is no nastiness. There is no shouting. There is no ill-will. There is nothing in the least bit negative. It couldn't be simpler.

Stage 3 – Use the quadrants as your basic language about behaviour

Identify the quadrant (or level) that the behaviour falls in. This, of course, refers to good behaviour as well as that which is unacceptable. Remember that the aim is to raise responsible teenagers. They need to know when they are being responsible as well as when they are falling short of the standards. It is just as important to praise and celebrate the good as it is to correct the unacceptable.

Offering praise or celebration

You can simply point out that you recognize the achievement of the higher levels of behaviour:

'Hey, Corrine. Top-right.'

'Oh, well done, Jerry. Quadrant D.'

'You can be proud of yourself staying in C and D all day, son. I can see how you're growing up.'

And so forth, are all perfect. They show that you appreciate the achievement without going over the top or gushing excessive praise. They are simple, easily understood and to the point.

If you want to offer more material recognition, there's no problem with that, but it shouldn't happen every time. The important thing to be careful of is that the reward doesn't become an implicit bribe. You don't want your teenager to be thinking, 'Hey, if I'm good, I'll get a reward.' Rather the motivation should be, 'Hey, if I'm good, I'm really demonstrating that I'm growing into a responsible person.' The primary reward that your teenager should have and treasure is a simple self-pride in doing the right thing simply because it is the right thing to do.

> The ultimate goal is responsibility because responsibility is the ultimate goal!

Offering reprimand

This is simply achieved by *asking questions*. It must be that your teenager is asked to think about and analyse (a) his own behaviour, and (b) what adjustments need to be made to show responsibility.

It is not your job to offer reprimand by pointing out that behaviour falls short of the standards. If you do this, you are doing the thinking and your teenager perceives it as nagging. Neither of these is a constructive approach.

If the problem is a minor one, the solution also needs to be pretty minor. You don't want to be bringing out the biggest guns for the smaller targets. You simply need to offer a gentle reminder about the quadrants and which quadrant behaviour you are looking for. In the case of major problems, the system can be used in a rather more formal way.

'Stuart, can you show me what Quadrant D behaviour looks like?'

'What does Quadrant D homework look like, Frank?'

'John? On what level is that behaviour?'

'What quadrant does shouting at me fall into, Sam?'

'What do you need to do to get into an adult quadrant, Amie?'

You can see it, can't you? You aren't criticizing. You aren't nagging. You are cool and calm and you're asking your teenager to think about what is and isn't appropriate behaviour.

Your teenager will hear the question and question himself. 'Why am I behaving in this way? Is it going to get me what I want to get? Am I showing that I am capable of behaving like and being treated like an adult? How should I be behaving?

What is an adult way of getting what I want? How would an adult behave in this situation?'

In most cases, this simple questioning is quite enough to change low-level behaviour into high-level behaviour. Your teenager will immediately see that the behaviour is immature and that failure to achieve adulthood is the obvious result. If an immediate move into quadrant D doesn't happen, then you need to escalate the system. This is dealt with in the next section, Rewards and Sanctions.

If a civil answer is not forthcoming, you have a clear indication that your teenager is well into ANGRY CHILD and this needs to be dealt with. You may want to refer back to Chapter 4 When Communication Gets Difficult (pp. 40–52) to remind you of how to deal with this. Your teenager wants to be adult, but doesn't always know what adulthood means. This is a gentle way of allowing her to think about it rather more deeply and to come to conclusions that are more positive.

Rewards and sanctions

You are the parent. You have the ultimate responsibility for bringing up your teenager. It is for you to set appropriate limits, rewards and sanctions. Having said that, your teenager is no longer a child, unquestioning and accepting of all that you say. Limits, rewards and sanctions need to be discussed and agreed. If they are, you will be helping your teenager develop an understanding that life has these things in place. If you impose punishments or tell your teenager what will and won't happen, your teenager will feel disempowered and helpless. This is a sure recipe for irresponsibility.

Human beings are complex creatures and their behaviour is no less complex. There are always going to be times when we behave in ways that are exceptional. Your teenager is always going to behave better than expected at times and worse at other times. When the behaviour is exceptionally good, it is perfectly reasonable and right to want to give rewards in recognition of this. At the odd times when behaviour falls short of expected standards, it is only right to recognize this as well. This recognition will depend very much on the behaviour.

Rewards

The purpose of a reward is to recognize and celebrate growing maturity and responsibility and to thank your teenager for something special. It is *never* to be used as a bribe or an inducement to meet expected standards. The main point to bear in mind is that rewards are not promised in advance, nor even hinted at. If they are, they become bribes and counter-productive.

You can choose the rewards according to your means. Usually, a simple verbal thanks and realistic recognition of success are all that is required. You might choose to have a special treat out to Macdonalds or The Ritz or maybe buy a CD or a new car, depending on the thickness of your wallet. The main reward that your teenager should get is the self-knowledge and self-esteem that tells her she is growing up to be a decent, honest, reliable and responsible person. Any reward that you choose to give is the icing on that already large and succulent cake.

Sanctions

The purpose of a sanction is not to punish. The sole purpose is to give your teenager the opportunity to come to two important realizations that are vital for developing responsibility.

The first realization is that consequences follow the actions that cause them. Good consequences follow good actions. Unwanted consequences follow unwanted actions. This is a natural law and no amount of disliking it is going to change it. These consequences fall into two distinct categories. There are natural consequences and social consequences.

Natural consequences are those that follow from natural laws. If you don't eat, you get hungry. If you eat the wrong amount of the wrong types of food, you get overweight or underweight. If you don't get enough high-quality sleep, you will be tired the next day. There is no great problem there. As long as your teenager is not suffering from any serious 'stinking thinking', they can certainly accept this, but they might not like it.

Social consequences follow from the fact that society has certain expectations and that when these expectations are not met, society imposes consequences. If you don't do your homework, you will get detention. If you steal, you will be known as a thief and not liked by decent people. If you are rude and aggressive, decent people will avoid you.

The second realization is that there is always a price to pay for irresponsible behaviour and that it is always extracted from the doer. This is another way of saying: 'You cannot break the rules. You can only break yourself against the rules.'

If misbehaviour causes upset to others, the price that responsible people pay is to make a heartfelt apology and a promise of change in the future. As a simple example, if playing music disturbs the neighbours and causes them upset, an immediate apology and a promise to play the music quietly in future must be made.

If misbehaviour causes damage to property, the price to be paid is to make full restitution and replace or repair the damaged property. A simple example of this is if a window is broken by a carelessly kicked ball, the cost of repair must fall on the person who broke it. It is not good enough to say, 'The insurance will pay for it.'

These two examples are simply natural justice in action. You could almost say that responsibility is little more or less than a profound understanding of natural justice. Justice is concerned with the way that people behave with each other and towards property, so it is a pre-requisite of a democratic society and of democratic behaviour.

At times of irresponsible behaviour, your primary job is to allow your teenager to come to the realization that their behaviour is unacceptable and to consider deeply:

- why it is unacceptable;
- how to avoid repeating it in the future;
- how recompense may be made.

It is a fundamental belief that change only ever comes from the inside and can never be imposed from the outside. You cannot force your teenager to behave responsibly; all you can hope to do is to provide him with the tools to change himself.

As the great Dr Stephen Covey wrote, 'People cannot live with change unless there is a changeless core inside them.'

81

What he meant by this is that your teenagers need to develop a changeless core of responsibility, goodness and decency. Your job, then, is to provide the opportunity for your teenager to develop this changeless core of responsibility for themselves. This is the only way that responsibility can possibly be developed – from the inside out.

There is a simple and unchanging technique for changing unwanted behaviours, and the clue is in the three bulleted points above.

- Question the level or quadrant of the behaviour.
- Question what changes need to be made to move into the high-level or D quadrant.
- Question how the offending behaviour can be avoided in future.
- Ask what recompense needs to be made.

Question the level or quadrant of the behaviour.

This is a simple and straightforward request for your teenager to look at his own behaviour through the eyes of other people. It is vital that he realizes that the way that he behaves will affect the way that other people behave towards him.

The next stage is to describe why the behaviour falls into that quadrant. It is important for your teenager to see the difference between quadrant A (= unthinking) behaviour and B (= thinking) behaviour.

Quadrant A is out of control. The solution to this behaviour pattern is to take control. The need is to develop self-control and realize that the two rules of respect and safety always apply to all people.

Quadrant B is deliberate naughtiness. The solution is to consider that other people's wants and needs have to be considered. The need is to develop self-respect and respect for others. The rules are already known, but flouted.

You can see how the distinction is really important. Without it, it is difficult for your teenager to see how to create a solution.

Question what changes need to be made to move into the high-level or D quadrant.

Once the behaviour is precisely described and understood, it is a fairly simple matter to see what changes need to be made. These need to be spelled out in precise detail. The changes will depend on whether the behaviour was in quadrants A or B.

Question how the offending behaviour can be avoided in future.

Now is the time for the deepest thought. When the same situation is met in the future, as it surely will be, what will your teenager do differently to avoid causing conflict, upset or damage? This is the time for a really deep emotional investment and commitment to making changes in behaviour patterns.

Let's get one thing clear. Changes *must* be made in order to develop responsibility, and they can only come from inside your teenager and will only be effective if they are seen on the outside in changed behaviour. It's for this reason that your teenager must think deeply about these things. It requires a mental rehearsal so that when the situation arises, the appropriate behaviour is already programmed.

Ask what recompense needs to be made.

As indicated earlier, natural justice requires that recompense be made for any problems caused by low-level behaviour. This is a vital part of responsibility: facing up to the realities of life. You need to ask your teenager what an appropriate recompense might be. You will usually find that the suggested recompense is stronger than one that you would impose. If the suggestion that you get is not acceptable, you must use your authority as parent to point this out as being insufficient. Eventually, you will reach an agreement.

Some possible recompenses are:

- A heartfelt verbal apology and promise to avoid the behaviour in future.
- A written apology (including details and a plan, if necessary).
- Loss or reduction of personal privileges (pocket money, TV time, evenings out and so forth) for an agreed time.
- Extra chores.
- Full financial restitution (or agreed restitution in kind, if the financial burden is too great) in the case of damage to property.

Remember during this stage that you are always looking for a Win-Win situation. You teenager must not feel that he is being punished by you wielding your authority. That will only lead to negative thoughts and resentment which will destroy any growth towards responsibility. It really does need to be an agreed recompense that enables your teenager to accept the responsibility for himself.

You can see that your teenager really needs to make a strong emotional investment in order to come to these decisions. It isn't easy to accept responsibility and no one is saying that it is easy. What I am saying is that it is necessary. Without this emotional investment, that unchanging centre is simply not going to be created. Never forget to praise your teenager for facing up to responsibility. Be stern, by all means, but be gracious and loving as well.

Emotions

As I said above, emotions are an important part of our human make-up and personality. There is no benefit in hiding them. Apart from anything else, hiding emotions is dishonest and doesn't lead to the good inter-personal relationships that breed responsibility. We need to make a clear distinction between emotional honesty and emotional blackmail. The first one is healthy; the second one is unhealthy and irresponsible.

Emotional honesty

It is both childlike and adult to be open and honest about emotions. It's only adolescents that sometimes find it difficult to express themselves emotionally. Teenagers get the idea that emotions are for the immature and not for the emerging adults that they are. That they so frequently make immature displays of inappropriate emotions is one of life's great mysteries!

There is nothing wrong with expressing emotions. We are all emotional beings and we all share the ability to feel the whole range of emotions. You must be emotionally honest with your teenager and encourage her to be emotionally honest with you. Teenagers spend so much time in emotional turmoil that is quite unnecessary. All they need is an openness and a safe environment to express themselves.

Emotional blackmail

This is quite a different animal. Emotional blackmail is using other people's emotions to your own ends and is immature. A typical example of emotional blackmail is, 'If you really loved me, you'd ...'

The thing you'd do can vary from letting your teenager stay up to watch a particular programme to allowing your thirteen-year-old daughter to go on holiday with her eighteen-year-old boyfriend.

Other more subtle versions exist. 'Jemima's parents let her go out to discos where alcohol is sold', 'Ralph stays up until midnight every night. Why can't I?', etc.

Teenagers have had a lifetime's experience of manipulating parents in this sort of way. It started the moment after birth when a wild, heart-rending cry made Mum place the newborn on the breast and has been carefully developed since.

You can use emotional blackmail to your advantage!

Rather than pointing out that Jemima isn't your daughter, you can allow the discussion to flourish. Ask if this is wise. Question deeply if this shows that Jemima's parents are really doing the best for their daughter. You can certainly point out that it seems unwise to you and then ask why you might think this.

Most teenagers will understand, eventually, that the limits that you place are there for a good reason – her continued safety and happiness. It can only help for her to understand this.

Anger

You wouldn't dream of hiding your joy at exceptionally good behaviour, so why hide anger? It is a perfectly normal and justifiable human emotion and denying the existence of any emotions is quite unhealthy. What you do need to do is to avoid allowing your anger to hijack your behaviour and losing control of yourself.

'Anyone can become angry – that is easy. But to be angry at the right person, to the right degree, at the right time, for the right purpose and in the right way, this is not easy.'

Aristotle

It is perfectly reasonable to let your teenager know that her behaviour can lead to anger in other people and that she needs to learn to avoid doing this. Making Mum angry may lead to tears and an upset mum. Making an aggressive person in a pub angry might well lead to a broken glass in the face.

Review

- Responsibility is the ability to choose the right response to any situation.
- Behaviour can be described in terms of acceptable or unacceptable, conscious or unconscious.
- Responsibility is unconscious acceptable behaviour – described as democratic.

Action Exercises

- Learn and teach the 4 Quadrants of Behaviour. Use them as your family's language. Guide your teenagers towards democracy.

- Use rewards and sanctions sparingly. Rewards should come as a pleasant surprise and never be used in advance as a bribe. Sanctions should be discussed using the Win-Win criteria.

- Raise your teenager's responsibility by helping him or her face up to any misdeeds and make full reparation. Give lashings of love and praise when this happens.

- Be open and honest about emotions, but don't get hijacked by anger.

EIGHT

Motivation

Start with the end in mind

Some time ago, I got a phone call from a worried parent. She told me: 'I need to know how to make my son succeed at school.' She immediately realized what she had said and corrected herself: 'I mean I need to know how to help him, not make him' and we both laughed. She understood that you can't easily make anybody do anything, and you can help them do things that they want to do.

One thing in life is certain. There are always forces that control. We can choose what these forces are. We can either allow things and events to control us or we can take control of things and events for ourselves. This is true of simple things like homework. If your teenager doesn't take control of the homework, then the homework will be in control. We've all experienced a frustrated teenager struggling with a seemingly impossible homework or coursework and being wound up into a terrible state. It's true of life in general. If your teenager doesn't take control of things, then things will control your teenager.

John LeCarre has a wonderful metaphor which I often use. A character in one of his books was describing someone as a little ship. When questioned about what he meant, he explained that little ships get carried by natural forces. They drift with the current and get blown off course by wayward winds. Big ships, on the other hand, can go where they want. They have the power to overcome untoward forces and can sail into the wind or with the wind as they wish. They can also sail with or against the prevailing currents and tide. Your teenager can choose to be a big ship and go to any place against any force, or he can choose to be a little ship and get driven wherever life's forces direct. The thing that controls the size of your teenager's ship is motivation and action.

There are four simple little sentences which liberate life's forces and direct them. They are simply:

- Have a good reason;
- Have a good plan;
- Do the right thing; and
- Do the thing right

These four little sentences cover both motivation and action.

Have a good reason

Everything that you do is done for a reason. It may be conscious or unconscious, but the reason is there. If you go to the bathroom, there's a reason and you don't need me to tell you what it is. If you feel down or depressed, there's a reason for it. If your teenager is going to be motivated to do the things that are going to lead to success in school and life, there has got to be a good reason for them to do so.

Now some people are motivated by moving toward success and others are motivated by moving away from failure. It's not really that important what your teenager's motivating force is – there is nothing that you can do about it anyway. It just seems to be a natural part of each individual's personality. The important thing is to move. The only way to move is to apply motivating forces, and that's what this is about. There are two stages to developing a good reason for success. The first is to have a dream – a wild and wonderful dream of what success means. The next stage is to create a solid vision.

Dream

Sit down and talk with your teenager. Talk about what real life is like and about real people that you know, as well as some you don't know personally but know of. Talk about people you know who have been really successful in their lives and some who have not had the success that they should have had. Your family, circle of friends and neighbourhood will contain many such people. Talk about them frankly and see what lessons can be learned from them.

You can also talk about people that you know of who have been successful. Sportsmen and women are a rich source for this. You can talk about how David Beckham and Venus Williams didn't just wake up one morning and find that they were world-class athletes. They got to the top having a dream and then going out and making that dream a reality. Discuss how there were many stages they had to go through and that there were probably many disappointments on the way. But the thing that they had to have in place first was that dream and the dream was the thing that helped them along the way.

Talk about the things that really fire up your teenager – those that get a real enthusiasm and light up the eyes. Talk about how these things can be a regular part of life only if you take control of life.

Help your teenager to dream big dreams. These should be dreams about the world of work, relationships, lifestyle, leisure activities and all the other things that go to make up a wonderful and exciting life. Encourage a real wild and wacky dream and come up with ideas of your own. Remember that your teenager doesn't have anything like your experience and probably can't see all the wonderful possibilities that life has to offer. You'll need to get into a dreamlike state yourself to help. This should be a meaningful and emotionally moving experience for both of you. The brain remembers emotions very strongly so you should encourage this emotional involvement.

Remember that the dream doesn't need to be practical. Resist any temptation to get into practicality or tell your teenager that such things aren't possible. Help them to understand that *anything* is possible for anyone. The dream isn't intended to be practical – it's only intended to open up your teenager's eyes to the wonderful opportunities that are available to people who have dreams.

Vision

The second stage is to take that wild and wonderful dream and put it into a solid form. This step is absolutely essential. Dreams have a nasty habit of evaporating in the cold, clear light of day and they can easily be forgotten. Visions, on the other hand, are the things that drive people to create lives of real success. You can easily imagine that there were thousands of university students in the early 70s who dreamed about setting up their own computer businesses. Bill Gates and Steve Jobs went beyond that stage. They had vision; and that vision led to success. Richard Branson is one of many thousands of young men who had dreams of success. You only need to look at his business empire now to see that he also has vision.

Vision is a dream with muscles and it's the written word that puts the muscles in place, builds them up and keeps them well exercised and well toned.

Some time after creating that dream, maybe immediately afterwards, sit down with your teenager and get it down on paper. There are many ways of doing this. You might want to create a concept map, get it written in the form of a 'Letter to Myself' or in a journal. Of these, I always recommend a simple undated journal or even an A4 notebook. This is flexible and can include anything. The only vital thing is that the dream gets written down in a form that your teenager can refer to again and again.

Remember the beginning of the chapter. You can't make your teenager succeed, but you can help. The vital first stage is to help create this vision.

Have a good plan

The biggest and brightest vision in the world isn't going to be much use without a plan to make it a reality. There is a saying: 'Failing to plan is like planning to fail.' No-one actually plans to fail, but most people fail to plan. It is this failure to plan that prevents most people from having the success that they could have. Without a plan, it is simply impossible to get the job done.

If you wanted to start a business, you'd first create a business plan. As long as your plan was clear and realistic and you followed it, your business would likely succeed. If the plan was not clear or you didn't take any notice of it, your business would almost certainly fail. Life is also like that.

The way that most teenagers find it quite easy to plan is to make a life plan, then divide life up into sections and create a sub-plan for each section. The life plan should include most of the major aspects of life and include details of how the major goals will be achieved. I then recommend that three sub-plans be made. A ten-year plan, a five-year plan and then a year plan. The longer term plans don't need to be very detailed, but more and more details need to be added as the term of the plan gets shorter. The year plan should be very detailed.

Teenagers are self-conscious and intensely interested in their own lives. They will really enjoy setting themselves up a plan in this way. The best way of making the plan is to keep a journal. The first section will be a description of their vision. The next few pages will be for the life plan, ten-year plan and so forth down to a detailed year plan. The rest of the journal can then be used as a diary to keep a record of life's happenings and how your teenager helps or hinders the plan's progress.

Napoleon Hill studied the lives of the USA's greatest industrialists of the early decades of the 1900s. He noted that they all kept journals. They used these journals as a way of sorting out their own lives and seeing what lessons needed learning. They recorded their successes and failures and made a special effort to learn from both. Hill came to the opinion that the single greatest secret of success was constantly learning life's lessons. If it worked for the likes of Henry Ford and Andrew Carnegie, it will work for your teenager.

Do the right thing

If you bake a cake and get the temperature of the oven wrong, your cake is going to come out wrong. The right results only ever flow from the right actions. This isn't a lesson that teenagers are terribly good at learning. They simply haven't yet developed the thinking skills that allow them the flexibility to look at results and actions and draw the right conclusions.

You'll see lots of evidence of this. Everything is someone else's fault. 'The teacher picks on me.' 'Someone else got me into trouble.' 'It fell apart in my hands.' 'It was Fred's fault. He started it.' 'You didn't get my games kit ready for me.' The list goes on and on and you know all about it if you've got a teenager. Just sit back for a moment and think of all the excuses you've heard over the years. Each and every one of them is an example of this thinking. Teenagers really do need a lot of help with this. They need to learn to look at themselves, the things that they do and the results that they get. It means developing sensitivity to others and self-responsibility.

Your teenager's journal is the key to sorting out this thinking and getting good thinking in place. It can be used for planning the right things to do and it can be used for understanding why things went wrong. It's used for looking forward to what life could be like and looking backwards at what life was like. We'll deal with this a little bit later in more detail, but the basic idea is: Think; Do; Think. It means think about the future and plan it, live it to the full and then learn the lessons so you live it even better in future.

Teach your teenager to plan the things he or she wants to do. Encourage good thinking about what the future should hold and how to make these things come true. Show how to ask the right questions: What do I really want out of life? What are the options? How am I going to get it? What do I need to do? How do I need to do it? What help do I need from other people? How can I persuade other people to help me get what I want? It's only by asking these questions and then finding the right answers that your teenager is going to get the good results in life.

If you look at these things, they are the questions that you, as an adult, ask yourself all the time. You've probably been doing these things for years and don't even think about them any more. You'll also see that it's only by getting answers to them that you know how to behave and what to do in new situations. Remember that your teenager hasn't had your years of experience and simply doesn't understand the way that real life works. Your teenager may well be streetwise, but I can guarantee that they aren't life-wise. That's simply because they haven't lived enough of it yet to get life wisdom.

Of course, the only way that you and I and any other adult

gained life wisdom is by making mistakes and learning the lessons! There is a saying: 'Good judgement is the result of learning from mistakes. And mistakes come from bad judgements.' There are lots of mistakes to be made in life, and your teenager will probably make most of them during their teenage years. That's not a problem – it's life. It seems that we have to go through these experiences in order to learn and grow. By far the fastest way of learning from mistakes is to face up to them and this, again, is where the journal comes in.

I sometimes hear the complaint that this approach to life is boring; it reduces spontaneity and creativity. The complaint is quite unfounded. True creativity and creative spontaneity are based strongly on discipline and disciplined living. Just think about any truly creative person you know. You'll find that they have a definite direction for their creativity to take them and they are always progressing. Without this basis, life doesn't have any consistent direction and it's like a little ship. Think about the people you know who don't have a direction. You'll see exactly what I mean.

Do the thing right

We all know of people who seem to do everything right, but they just don't get the success they appear to deserve. The problem always lies in one of two areas. Either they don't bring the right attitude to the job or they don't bring enough quality to it. There are two aspects to doing the thing right. The first is that it's done with a positive mindset and the other is that the job is done with a quality mindset. Of course, the two go very much hand in hand.

There's a lot of talk these days about self-esteem and how important it is to us all. It's quite right. If we don't have a high degree of self-esteem then it's difficult to bring a positive mindset to anything. The question is: where does self-esteem come from?

Your teenager has to understand the idea that if a job's worth doing, it's worth doing well and get into the habit of setting him- or herself high-quality standards. This applies to homework, coursework, personal grooming and family relationships – in fact any and every area of life. The answer to the question: 'Where does self-esteem come from?' is that it comes from seeing the good results from good actions. And good results only ever come from a conscious decision to do the right thing and then doing the thing right.

You know the refrain of the old song, 'It ain't what you do, it's the way that you do it. That's what gets results.' Well, it's true. Attitude is everything, and it's attitude as much as anything else that gets people known. Again, teenagers need a lot of help with this one.

If there is one thing which is absolutely guaranteed to turn people off and make sure that your teenager doesn't get the results that will benefit him or her, it's a bad attitude. No-one likes it and it never gets cooperation and help. It can often turn people away from offering help when they would otherwise have done so. Being well motivated and having a clear vision of what life should and could be like will almost guarantee that your teenager has a wonderful attitude to life. And it is this, and only this, which will get the positive results that he or she wants.

Teenagers have to learn one of life's most essential lessons: you have to get along with other people in order to get on in life and enjoy success. Again, your teenager's personal journal is the key to getting this mindset fixed.

Review

- Motivation depends on having a clear vision of the future as you would like it to be and a good plan to get there. After that, it's a case of working towards that future.
- Keeping a journal is an excellent way of staying on track for goals.

Action Exercises

- Teach your teenager the four secrets: Have a good reason; Have a good plan; Do the right thing; and Do the thing right. Talk about these things and see how they apply to everything of any value.
- Buy your teenager a journal.

94

NINE

The Time of Your Life

Start with the end in mind

Your teenager has got a life to live and that life is lived in time. Just look around you at the people that you know. You'll always find that those who spend their time doing a variety of different things are the happiest and most interesting people. Well, it's just like that for your teenager. The simple fact is that the more things that your teenager can pack into life, the happier he or she will be.

There is a saying: 'variety is the spice of life' and your teenager wants a well-spiced life. So help him or her to get as much variety into it as possible. Yes, of course, your teenager is a school teenager. But he or she is also a family teenager and a friend teenager as well as being a sports teenager and a private-person teenager. All these things are just as important. All work and no play makes for a dull life. All play and no work makes for an unproductive life.

The key element in an enjoyable life is balance in all things. The only way to ensure that life is balanced is to design it to allow enough time for everything. It's not only money that is a good servant and a bad master. Exactly the same is true of time.

Slow and steady loses the race

The old saying 'slow and steady wins the race' might be true in a race between a tortoise and a hare in *Æsop's Fables*, but it simply isn't true for the human race. Look at the story carefully. You'll notice that the only reason the tortoise won is because of the stupidity of the hare. Relying on someone else's stupidity to allow you to win isn't going to pay off most of the time. It's an excellent recipe for losing! There are certainly times when a cautious approach to some things works best, but generally 'go for it' is a better approach.

Winners are winners because they have a great race plan, prepare themselves well, and then go out and give a first-class performance. That's also the way that your teenager is going to be one of life's winners.

Helen Keller wrote, 'Life is a daring adventure or it is nothing at all.' The way to make life an adventure is to make it fast and furious and to live it to the full. There is no time for just sitting round and stooging and being bored. In truth, there are no boring things, only bored people. The way out of boredom is not to allow it into life in the first place.

Divide up your life

Anyone's life, especially that of a teenager, is made up of many different parts. Just look at yourself. You're a parent, a friend and socializer, probably a breadwinner, a nurse, a coach, a family teacher and mentor. The list goes on and on, and it is the same for your teenager. The secret to living a happy life is getting as much into life as possible. Help your teenager to use time wisely and to allow enough time for each of the important things in life. There are three stages to this process.

The first stage is to look at life and help your teenager to decide what his or her major life roles are. You have to look at the categories and simplify them to keep things manageable. For example, your teenager is a son or daughter, maybe a brother or sister, nephew or niece, and so on. This is just too much to handle. Condense them all down into one broad category called Family Member. The ideal number of life roles is about five or six. Here are some suggestions:

- Family Member
- Friend and Socializer
- Student

- Sportsman/woman
- Private Person

The second stage is to draw a pie chart and divide it up into slices representing each of the life roles. The size of the slice depends on the relative importance of each of the roles. There will probably be many attempts before you get this right. It's not an easy thing even for adults to do. It's going to be a rather difficult personal decision, and there's no problem with that. Teenagers have to learn to do these things and now is a good time to start. Here's an example.

My Time

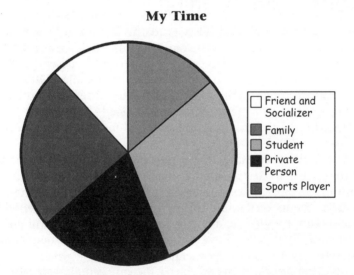

Your teenager's pie chart will reflect his or her own individual ideas and tastes. There is no single balance that is ideal for everyone. You can certainly give a little help but you mustn't interfere and tell your teenager what to do. That would destroy the point of the exercise. No one develops responsibility by being told what to do.

I'd recommend that no less than four hours a week is dedicated to schoolwork, and that six hours or more is more realistic. Some of this time is going to be for assigned homework and coursework. Some of it is going to be for private study. If this time is not put in, you can guarantee that the results at school will be less good than they should be. The only way to get the job done is commit to it, and the only way to commit to it is with time. There is always a price to be paid. The price of successful study is sufficient effective study time.

The third stage is to decide how many non-school hours there are in life and to design an outline timetable. As a rough guide, there are probably five 'disposable hours' each weekday evening and maybe twelve each weekend day. That gives a total of about fifty hours. Now your teenager can make a sensible estimate of how he or she should be spending this time.

Long-term planning

Now that your teenager has a pretty good idea of how much time each life role is worth, you can start looking at how to make sure that each one gets the time that it deserves. The way to do this is to make a weekly timetable. This is a personal thing and will depend on many different factors. If there is a favourite TV programme, it needs to be taken into account. Also, sports clubs and youth clubs and the like must be included.

The skill of creating this type of timetable is to get the things with fixed times in first. Decide then on the most important ones that have to be fitted in with other people. Finally, the more flexible things get slotted in to convenient times. Don't expect to be able to create a timetable quickly and easily. There will have to be a lot of rearrangements and changes before a perfect timetable is made.

It's also important to realize that no one is making a tool to beat your teenager up with. If it doesn't seem to be working out as planned, feel free to make changes as necessary. The end result must be something that everyone feels comfortable with. As a simple example, if a new TV programme starts and it interferes with a homework night, make the change. Move some things around to allow for new situations.

This is a perfect opportunity for you to help your teenager develop responsibility for two things. First of all, he or she has to make some decisions about what life should look like. Secondly, there is the self-discipline to stick to those decisions. Both of those are character-building exercises. Naturally, there are going to be times when problems arise. What you have to do is help your teenager realize that life is like this sometimes and that flexibility and commitment is needed. No-one can have it all and life, to some extent, is always a compromise.

Once the long-term planning is in place, the short-term, day-to-day living is easily taken care of.

Long-term study planning

Examinations are a regular part of school life and have to be taken seriously. Sadly, this is something that most students simply don't do until the last minute. This creates two problems. First of all, it makes sure that they get lower grades than if they'd started studying earlier. Secondly, it makes examinations incredibly stressful.

The simple fact is that learning is a process, not an event. The only way to learn well is to do it over an extended period. The technique of coasting and cramming is the most ineffective study method imaginable. Think of examinations as being like an athletic event. Athletes don't just sit around for most of the year and then start training just before a big meeting. They are constantly training at a level that keeps

Paced Work

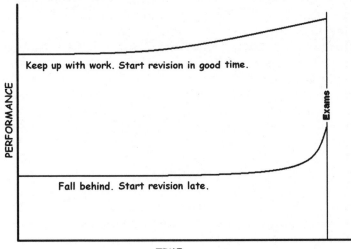

99

them in good condition. Then, as the big event starts getting closer, they accelerate their training. They know that they need to be at peak performance at just the right time.

It's exactly the same with study. To get the best exam results your teenager needs to study at a good enough level to keep on top of the work. Slipping behind for any reason is going to cause problems. Then, some time before exams start, make a gently accelerating revision plan and stick to it. The idea is, just like an athlete, to reach peak performance just at the right time. Doing this, your teenager will 'Go for Gold' and get the best grades possible.

This graph shows well what happens. When the work is learned steadily, there is an excellent basis for revision. If there is a constant slipping behind, there is nothing to build revision on. This is wasteful of time and stressful.

Single-time learning is possible for things which are absolutely fascinating and emotionally interesting. This is not true for most school learning! To be quite honest, a lot of the stuff your teenager needs to learn isn't all that gripping. But it still needs to be learned! The only way to get the learning really solid is by constant revision. The graph shows how it works.

Revision

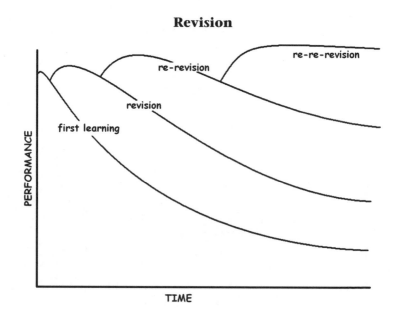

Most learning is forgotten within twenty-four hours or so. To make sure that this doesn't happen, a quick five-minute revision of yesterday's work is all that is needed. This alone will significantly increase the amount remembered. Five minutes of revision a week later can better memory yet again. A quick review a few weeks later and the work is well consolidated.

The way to do this is to spend about fifteen to twenty minutes each day looking over yesterday's work, last week's work, last month's work, and so forth. You can see how this makes a *huge* difference to the amount of learning that gets done. And it's a much more productive use of time than stewing in front of the TV all evening.

This simple system saves time and stress. It saves time because revision before examinations is really simple. Most students go through a cycle of learning, forgetting and relearning just before exams and then forgetting again immediately after exams. This system makes sure that learning is kept at a high level all year and that final revision is polishing an already well-polished knowledge base. You can also see how it relieves the stress of exams. Instead of your teenager going through a month of uncontrolled panic, he or she knows that they have a really strong knowledge base to work from and that revision is not such a big problem. The time problem and the stress problem are both solved by the same simple system.

Short-term study planning

Let's get one thing clear right at the beginning. Long, unproductive study sessions are boring and self-defeating. If your teenager doesn't enjoy studying and doesn't get any reward from it, then study simply won't get done. Oh, yes, there might be time spent, but there won't be much learning going on. We all know what the result of this will be. There's stomping around the house, constant complaints and whining 'I can't do it,' or, 'What's the point anyway?' and a generally bad atmosphere. It doesn't have to be like that.

The secret to effective study is to work with the brain instead of against it. The brain just loves being focused on a task and learning new things. If this focus isn't there or the learning doesn't come, the brain gets bored and looks for something else to do. This means that study has to be fast and focused. It's basic biology and no amount of wishing it to be otherwise is going to change it. Bullying your teenager into going into his or her room to study for hours on end is pointless. It's just about the most counter-productive thing that you could possibly do.

The graph below shows what happens. A long study session quickly gets boring and concentration falls to a low level. You know this feeling yourself. If you've ever read a boring book, you know that you can finish several pages and not remember a single thing. Your eyes wander off the page and you find yourself losing your place. It's terrible and a complete waste of time and effort.

The way out of this is to plan several micro sessions. Each one should be between twenty and twenty-five minutes long. Much less than this and the brain doesn't focus. Much more and boredom sets in. Each session should be separated by a break of five minutes or so just to limber up the body and brain and ensure that both are comfortable.

Each of these micro sessions should be quite sufficient to do a single homework assignment. If homework regularly takes much more than this, the teacher should be consulted – there

Study Session

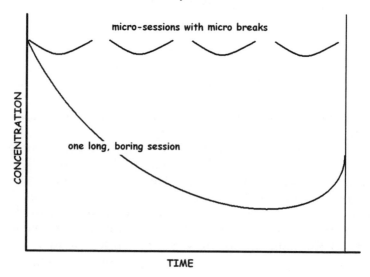

micro-sessions with micro breaks

one long, boring session

CONCENTRATION

TIME

is a problem somewhere and it needs to be sorted out. In the case of working on an extended task like coursework or a project, break the task up into sections. Then treat each of these sections as a separate task and fit each one into the system above.

Before sitting down to work, your teenager must know exactly what the job is. The plan needn't be detailed, or even written out. The only important thing is that there is a reason for doing the job. It's quite enough if your teenager can tell you, for example, 'I've got a history homework to do and an English essay to plan. Then I'm going to read ahead in physics and revise last week's work.'

Preparing to study

If you walked in to any modern mechanic's workshop you'd see immediately that tools and equipment are always neatly stored when not in use and available at a moment's notice. Mechanics haven't got time to waste and neither has your teenager. Time is far too precious to waste looking for things and getting frustrated when you can't find them. You'd also notice that the mechanics take a moment or two to analyse the job thoroughly before getting all the tools together and starting work. Teach your teenager to prepare equipment and books before starting work. (Just think of the huge advantage your teenager will have at that first interview. When he or she explains that they have excellent personal organization skills and know the value of preparation, they'll be streets ahead of the competition. Employers and universities want youngsters who know how to get the job done – and preparation is ninety per cent of the job.)

You probably know that the brain is divided into two hemispheres and that the right-hand part of the brain controls the left-hand part of the body and vice versa. The brain also uses fuels, just like the body. The brain needs plenty of oxygen and glucose from the blood, as well as plenty of water. To do good work and do it fast, your teenager needs to prepare his or her brain.

By far, the easiest way of doing this is going for a brisk walk just before starting a study session. Walking gets the blood oxygenated and helps mobilize glycogen from the liver and converts it into glucose. Because walking uses both sides of the body, it balances both sides of the brain, and this is essential for good learning. Walking also allows the opportunity for thinking out problems and planning.

Both a borrower and a lender be

There are always going to be times when things don't go according to plan and everything goes haywire for a while. As long as you have a good degree of flexibility in your system, this is easily dealt with. This is simply put in place by deciding to borrow time rather than steal it and keep the possibility of lending time in mind.

As an example: maybe the circus comes to town and the only tickets available are for a study night. It wouldn't really be fair or sensible to insist that study comes first and to miss the circus. That is not likely to lead to good relationships or productive study being done that night! If your teenager creates a time management system, it has to be seen as an aid to life not a straightjacket.

In a case like this, you would borrow time from another time slot (say Friends and Socializing or Family) and agree to swap over the two times. All you are doing is making a small adjustment to the timetable and making sure that you keep a good balance between the different life-roles. In the same way, you can help your teenager to see that it's perfectly possible to lend time ahead of time if it's going to be a benefit. Of course, it's only fair to pay back later time which is lent. This keeps everything equitable and on an even keel.

Review

- The teenage years can be a wonderful time if life is lived to the full. Make sure that this is done by paying full attention to every important part of life.
- Study is an important part of life, but it's not the be all and end all. Make sure that it is done effectively and efficiently with excellent planning. There's then plenty of time left over for friends, family and fun.
- Time is even more valuable than money. Use it just as wisely. Borrow and pay back time if you need to.

Action Exercises

■ Spend some time with your teenager and teach him how to divide up life so that everything gets taken care of.

■ Teach your teenager to plan long-term and short-term study time.

■ Encourage flexibility and balance where time is concerned.

Helping With Homework

Start with the end in mind

There can be few things more distressing than a teenager who has an impossible homework assignment to get in tomorrow and who can't do it. It's even worse in the later years when it comes to coursework for GCSEs and A levels. Anger, fear and frustration mount up, and the parents are the ones who bear the brunt of it. Most of the work is incomprehensible to many parents. The stuff we did in school is out of fashion and the skills needed by students these days are different. It's become so bad that even I, an ex-maths teacher, have to think deeply about some of my children's maths homework.

The problem has always been there, and has always had the same cause. Schools concentrate on the what rather than the how. School kids are taught what to learn, but not how to learn it. This is changing slowly, but most of it is too little, too late. You probably can't help your teenager much with the subject matter, but you can do a lot to help in other ways. There are a few practical things that you can do that make the situation much easier. You can also help your teenager to develop good working and thinking practices.

For the last few weeks, I've been working with a young girl in Year 11 taking her GCSEs in a few months. She was fearful and panic-stricken. Just after the mock exams, she could only see failure and no hope of a university place. After just a few hours of tutoring she is brighter and full of confidence that she will do well. I haven't taught her very much in the way of subject matter – she's taught herself all that. All I did was to show her how to get the job done. You can easily help your teenager do the same.

Time and place

Homework needs to be done regularly and your teenager needs to see it as a job and approach it in a business-like way. The time and the place for schoolwork need to be thoroughly prepared in advance. For youngsters in the lower school an hour a night, three nights a week is quite usual. In the later years, it may be quite a lot more.

You need to agree a timetable with your teenager that will allow for three things. First of all, it must allow for current work to be done. There is no question of allowing homework to slip behind. It is next to impossible to catch up, so don't fall behind in the first place. Secondly, last week's and last month's work should be revised. If revision isn't an ongoing thing, work gets forgotten. That means that there's a cycle of learning, forgetting and re-learning just before exams. This is inefficient and stressful. There should also be a little time for reading ahead. Lessons are learned much better if your teenager has an idea of what they are about before they start.

Imagine that you decide to build your own house and go along to an architect's office to talk about the plans. You walk in and see the architect lying on the floor sketching things out and there's loud rock music blasting out or a TV blaring away in the corner. All his equipment is scattered about on the floor. You would probably walk straight out again and look for another one – someone who looks business-like.

As you know, you would never see such a sight. An architect's office would be neat and tidy with everything ready to hand. The drawing board would be well lit and with a comfortable seat. The desk would be tidy and have a place for everything and everything would be in its place. If there is any music playing it would be quiet and relaxing. That describes what your teenager's working space should look like as well. Your teenager should work at a large enough desk or table to allow all their equipment to be laid out neatly and tidily. There should be plenty of light: preferably not fluorescent – halogen desk lights are ideal. It is tiring to work in a dimly lit place and your teenager will be yawning within minutes if he tries to work like this. The chair should be at the right height and give back support or be a kneeler type. Comfort is essential.

Many teenagers insist that they can only work when lying on the floor or a bed. Once they discover the improvements of sitting at a proper desk and how much faster and better they work, they never go back. If you do get any resistance, discuss it openly and honestly. Talk about the way real people work and why they work that way. Ask your teenager to humour you, try it with an open mind and then to give you an honest opinion at the end.

A word or two about music fits in well here. A huge amount of research has been done into learning and study. It's been found that the best mental state for learning is a state of relaxed awareness – almost a meditative state. Loud rock music is wonderful for the disco when you want to be leaping around and having fun but it's terrible for learning. Quiet classical or New Age music is relaxing and gets the brain into just the right restful state that is best for learning. You might have heard about the Mozart Effect. This is exactly what it is. I've worked with dozens of teenagers who have fought against this tooth and nail. They absolutely *have* to have loud music to work to, or so they tell me. Without a single exception, they have all told me that they work much faster and better to quiet music once they try it a couple of times.

The homework diary

Your teenager will certainly have a homework diary issued by the school. Many schools now have fancy diary-type planners instead which are a great improvement. Each time your teenager is given homework, the teacher will tell all the teenagers to take out their homework diaries and will tell them exactly what to write in them. The homework will always be set clearly. It is a part of every teacher's planning to make sure that homework is appropriate, useful and doable. This even has to be shown on the teacher's lesson plans which are inspected regularly. Each year group has a homework timetable which teachers must respect. Homework is usually set for handing in two or more days later. It is never set for the next day. If your teenager has a frantic rush to get it done for the next day, it's his fault, not the teacher's. (If it is the teacher that is setting homework for handing in the next day, a word needs to be had. This isn't the preferred way of doing things.)

Your teenager's form tutor will check the diaries at least once a week to make sure that they are being kept up to date. You should do the same. If a teacher doesn't set a homework for some reason one week, this should also be noted in the diary. In this way, the diary is always kept as an accurate record of homework or its absence.

Those schools that use planners instead of simple homework diaries usually have spaces for you to write comments and little notes to the teachers or your teenager's form tutor. Make full use of this. You might wish to comment that a homework was too easy or difficult, or even send a reason why it wasn't done if an emergency cropped up. Schools spend quite a lot of money on these diaries. Make the best use of them.

The kit

It's a good idea for teenagers to have two sets of kit. One set is kept in the school bag and the other is the homework kit. (My kids keep their homework kit in a shoebox.) Both sets of kit are maintained in good order. Each kit contains the same things:

- four colours of ball-point pen;
- two pencils;
- an eraser;
- a ruler;
- set squares;
- compasses;
- a calculator; and
- a dictionary.

Having this kit ready at home and ready at school saves a lot of time and makes for much better work being done. I don't allow my youngsters to use liquid paper, schools don't allow it and I advise that you don't either. If any corrections need to be made, a simple, neat line through the mistake and the correction written clearly is fine.

Just an observation, but it's always the weakest students who regularly turn up for class without proper equipment. Please don't allow your teenager to do this. It's a terrible start to any lesson and gives completely the wrong signal to the teenager himself. You wouldn't expect a service engineer to turn up to fix your boiler without the right tools; schools don't expect youngsters to turn up without their proper kit.

Getting the job done

Getting homework done means that your teenager's brain has got to be working in the best possible way. There is only one way to get the job done, that's to do it. There's only one way to get all of life's jobs done. That's to do them fast and well. This is how to help your teenager prepare his or her brain to get the jobs done better than he or she ever thought possible. This is a technique that I call Brain Magic.

Sit up straight

Like most people, you probably enjoy quiz shows on TV. Think back to your favourite quiz show and visualize it. Notice how the contestants are standing or sitting. Notice how upright they are. There's a light in their eyes and they look alert and 'in the moment'. The reason is obvious enough, isn't it? It's because they need to get the best access to their brains. They have a natural understanding that the brain is smart and tuned in when the body looks smart and tuned in.

In an upright position, breathing is deeper and therefore better. This means that more oxygen gets into the blood-stream and the brain. The blood also circulates better when upright, so the blood flows more easily to the brain. Being upright not only improves the circulation and the way you look and feel, it also improves thinking and learning speed and depth. You can teach this to your teenager. Help him or her to use this knowledge and get into a good mental state for learning at any time.

Relax

Relaxation is essential for good learning. The brain is made up of three main parts: they are (1) the brain stem; (2) the limbic system; and (3) the cerebrum.

3 parts of the brain

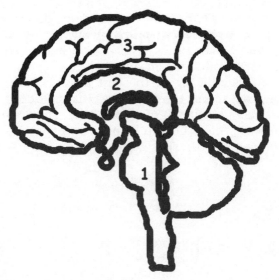

The brain stem (1) is the most primitive part of the brain. It controls basic functions like breathing, heartbeat, digestion and so forth, and the basic instincts of survival that we share with all animals. It is often called the reptilian brain, as it is almost identical to the brain of dinosaurs and modern-day reptiles. The limbic system controls emotions and parts of the memory. It is often called the brain's juice bar because it produces the 'happy juices' and 'stress juices' that control behaviour. The cerebrum (3) is the thinking brain. It is *huge* in humans – eighty percent of the brain's mass.

We are much nearer to our cave-dwelling ancestors than we suppose and our brains are designed more to aid in survival than to get GCSEs. When we are stressed, the limbic system produces stress juices that turn the cerebrum off and heighten the abilities of the brain stem. When your teenager gets into a bad mood, the thinking brain gets switched off and the reptilian brain takes over. So if your teenager sometimes goes snapping round the house like an angry crocodile, now you know why!

You have probably heard of brainwaves. These are tiny electrical signals that exist within your brain. No-one knows why they are there or what they actually do, but some interesting discoveries have been made. These brainwaves can be of a range of frequencies (given the names of Greek letters) from just a couple of cycles per second (Hz) up to forty or so Hz. The frequency of the brainwaves is strongly related to the level of arousal. High arousal, high frequency and vice versa. The mid-range frequencies of relaxation and awareness are good for learning and the others aren't.

Name	Frequency	Mental state	Learning?
Beta (β)	13–30 Hz	High arousal, everyday living	☹
Alpha (α)	7–12 Hz	Relaxed and aware	☺
Theta (θ)	4–6 Hz	Deep meditative state	☹
Delta (δ)	1–3 Hz	Sleep	☹

Focus

Have you ever tried talking to a carpenter or plumber when they are working in your house? If you have, you'll have noticed that they never carry on a conversation and work at the same time. When a carpenter, for example, is working on a piece of wood, his concentration is total. If it isn't, he'll probably hit his thumb with the hammer or take a slice out of his finger with a saw or chisel.

The only way to get the job done is to focus on it. Your teenager must learn that listening to raucous music, daydreaming or thinking about other things when studying is destructive as well as being a waste of time.

Auto-focus

Have you ever watched an athlete just before a big event and noticed what they do? They jump up and down a few times and shake their bodies to loosen their muscles. They breathe deeply to get plenty of oxygen into their bodies. They don't spend time chattering to each other – they are completely focused on the event. They are visualizing the race or whatever and playing it over and over in their minds.

What they are doing is getting into a delightful mental state called the flow state. Athletes usually call it the zone. It's a mental state in which everything flows naturally and easily. You can always tell when an athlete is in this state. Their performance looks effortless and almost dreamlike.

It's quite easy to get into this state when studying – and study becomes almost effortless and dreamlike. During this time a wonderful thing begins to happen without any effort. First of all, relaxation becomes a little deeper and brainwaves slow down to lie on the border between the alpha and theta states at about seven cps. Breathing slows, deepens, and switches to automatic belly breathing. As this happens, the left and right hemispheres of the brain come into balance and mental abilities rocket. Using both hemispheres of the brain rather than the usual one or the other brings an incredible intellectual boost. It can be compared to the difference between hopping on one foot and running.

Thinking it through

4-stage thinking system

Just a couple of weeks before writing this I was observing a Year 11 maths class. One of the students was having difficulty answering a question. The teacher was helping him out. I heard the teacher say, 'Come on, Sam. Think about it.' I could see what was going through Sam's mind. It was something like, 'If I knew how to think about it, I'd think about it and get on and do it.'

Sam's problem was that he didn't know how to think about the problem and come to a solution for himself. This is the most common problem that students have. I invented this system to overcome it. Teach this to your teenager and they will thank you for the rest of their lives. This system works perfectly for classwork, homework, coursework or sending rockets to Mars. And it only takes about five minutes to learn the basic ideas!

The system is:

- Think 1 – understand the problem
- Think 2 – plan how to find the answer
- Do – neatly and completely
- Review – check it and learn how to do it better and faster next time

It could hardly be simpler, could it? But there is more. It's not enough just to be told, for example, 'You must understand the question.' If you can't understand it, it's not much

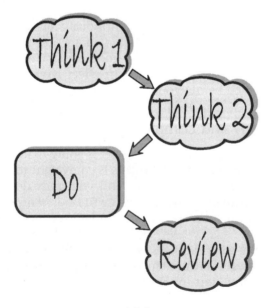

help. The system also includes strategies for doing all these things. We'll now look at the stages one-by-one and explain how to do each one.

Think 1 – understand the problem

You absolutely must understand a question before you can even hope to get a correct answer. It's a bit like making a mental map. Many youngsters simply don't know how to read a question. Here's the technique:

- Identify the key words
- Identify the key information
- Get the key ideas out of the brain
- Put them all together and explain the question to yourself in your own words.

Think 2 – plan how to find the answer

Planning how to find the answer is exactly the same idea as planning your route on a map. You need to know the start and end points and see the quickest and easiest route. You can immediately see the absolute necessity for having a clear mental map now, can't you?

Thinking out this plan is enormously de-stressing. You know at every stage exactly where you are and you will have either an exact knowledge or a good idea of what the part answer and full answer will be. In effect, you have got the problem solved before you have even started!

Do – neatly and completely

Now that you know what the answer is going to look like, you can get on and write it down. This is equivalent to travelling. Travellers often keep a journal, and you must do the same. When you write it down, you must write *everything* down! Not only that, it must be done neatly and correctly so that it can be read easily.

Go step-by-step. Going step-by-step ensures that you are not going to get out of step with your plan. If you think it, write it. If any step involves more than one process, write exactly what it is that you are using or doing. Leave yourself plenty of clues along the way. Show your thinking and understanding. Each and every step of the way must be shown. Having a systematic approach to writing out your working makes life so much easier for you and everyone else. Being lazy about this is not going to help anyone.

Review – check it and learn how to do it better and faster next time

This is the step that nearly all students miss out, and by doing this they reduce their ability to learn to a small fraction of what it should be.

Let's remember that the only result you are looking for is the perfect answer. You can only find this quickly and easily if you know what it is going to be before you start. That's exactly why you have to go through the process of understanding the question and planning the answer. The ideal to aim for is that you don't have to wait for the teacher or examiner to tell you if your answers are right or wrong. You should know this for yourself.

> You can find a full-colour e-book in PDF form on my website www.braintrainer.co.uk which explains this system. This download is free.

One of the first girls that I showed this system to amazed me. She was so emotionally confused that she was swinging between tears of joy and tears of anger. The joy was that finally, after ten and a half years of school, she could see exactly how to learn. The tears of anger were directed at her schools which had allowed her to struggle and fail for those ten and a half years.

Her mother, a debt counsellor, told me that she used exactly the same system at work without knowing it. Her first job was to find out why people got into debt. The second stage was to make a plan to eliminate the debt. The third stage was to support clients in their getting out of debt and then, finally, to help them stay out of debt.

This isn't just a system for studying. It's a system for living.

Review

- You may not be able to help with the subject matter of homework, but you can help enormously by teaching your teenager how to work properly.
- Help your teenager to work by preparing the space and time and preparing his or her brain.
- Teach your teenager how to think through problems and tasks: Think 1; Think 2; Do; Review.

Action Exercises

- Make sure that there is a neat, tidy, well-lit and comfortable place for homework to be done.

- Help your teenager develop good organizational skills.

- Teach your teenager to prepare physically and mentally before doing homework.

- Teach your teenager to: Think 1; Think 2; Do; Review.

ELEVEN

When Learning is Difficult

Start with the end in mind

When I was going home from London one evening I got chatting to someone on the train. He was an interesting man: an accomplished artist and photographer with exhibitions in London and a writer of short stories which he self-published. As we were chatting we got onto the subject of dyslexia. 'Oh, you don't believe in that, do you? It's just a nice word for stupidity,' he said. Here was an intelligent man who had the most incredibly profound misunderstanding of a common situation. He wasn't intentionally being offensive, he just didn't realize that he was being. Of course, he's not alone. Too many people think that giving special names to certain learning difficulties is just political correctness. They are wrong.

These things are very real. They have identifiable symptoms and physical causes and are just as real as a broken leg or a boil on the bum. That they are not as obvious at first glance or cause real physical pain is neither here nor there nor important. They are all caused by abnormalities in the brain. Different abnormalities to different degrees cause different symptoms in different people. There are a lot of 'differents' in that sentence, and there are a lot of differences in the way that these things show up. That is a big part of the problem.

There are no cures for specific learning difficulties (SLDs). And there are very many practical and quite simple things that can be done to help people with SLDs thrive in the teenage years and beyond. Some of these are things that the school can do and many more are things that you can do at home.

Please heed a word of warning. Don't read through this and jump to any hasty conclusions. Many of the symptoms described apply to perfectly normal people to a greater or lesser extent. Some people with the conditions exhibit only a few of the symptoms described. It isn't uncommon for two or more of these dysfunctions to exist at the same time. You can imagine that this makes diagnosis difficult. Identifying a single SLD can be quite difficult as no two cases are ever identical and the symptoms are not consistent. The difficulty is compounded if two or more dysfunctions are present.

You cannot and should not expect to come to any hard and fast conclusions from a short section in a short, non-specialist book like this. If you have any concerns, you should enquire either at school or consult your family doctor and have your teenager seen by a specialist. It is absolutely pointless sitting and worrying that there may be a problem. If you think that there may be, have it checked out. It may turn out to be something or nothing. If it is nothing, you can put your mind at rest and just get on with the job of raising your teenager. If it is something, then you can get all the expert help that you will almost certainly need.

Special needs

Youngsters with Special Educational Needs (SEN) are defined in law as being those who have learning difficulties that make it harder for them to learn than most children of the same age. The causes may be intellectual, physical, behavioural, social, emotional or developmental, or a combination of these. It may be that a child has problems with just one area such as reading and writing or maths, or may have across-the-board difficulties. You can see that with a broad definition like that, quite a few youngsters may be in need of special help at some time in their school career.

Schools have a legal obligation to provide suitable educational opportunities for all their pupils and this includes catering for SEN. Every school will have a Special Educational Needs Coordinator – always called SENCO – whose job it is to help identify and provide suitable education for these young-sters. These teachers are highly knowledgeable, skilled and dedicated people and do wonderful work. They are also universally easily approachable. If you need to talk to them, they will take time from their busy schedules and give you as much as they can. Please, out of respect and sympathy for their busy schedules, if you do need to talk, prepare yourself well and don't waffle!

If you feel that your teenager has SEN and these are not being met, contact the school immediately. The best way is probably to ask to speak to your teenager's form tutor and say what it is about. The form tutor will then set the wheels in motion for you and arrange for SENCO to be involved. SENCO will explain to you what the school can do and will guide you through the process.

Dyslexia

The old-fashioned name for dyslexia was word blindness. It wasn't a good name as it only described a small part of the symptoms. These days dyslexia is defined (by the WHO) as:

A disorder manifested by difficulty learning to read, despite conventional instruction, adequate intelligence and socio-cultural opportunity. It is dependent upon fundamental cognitive disabilities which are frequently of constitutional origin.

The usual understanding of this is that a child is dyslexic if his reading age is very much below his real age and he is of normal or above intelligence. It is a condition that existed at birth or was acquired shortly afterwards. It is *not* caused by ineffective teaching, social deprivation, lack of motivation or low intelligence. These things may lead to a reduced ability to read, but that is not the same thing as dyslexia.

Dyslexia is often considered to be a gift in life. It leads to a reduced ability to read well, and it often indicates particular strengths in other areas. Albert Einstein was probably the most famous dyslexic. He shared this gift with such people as Winston Churchill, George Washington, Mohammed Ali, Richard Branson, William Hewlett (of Hewlett Packard) and many other very successful people.

Although dyslexia has been studied for many years, no-one knows exactly what the causes are. There are almost as many opinions as there are experts. There are, however, a few things that are agreed on. Dyslexia is frequently associated with left-handedness and slowness in getting the job done. There are a few differences in brain structure that have been found regularly amongst dyslexics. Also, there seems to be some impairment of the transmission of information from the eyes to the brain.

There is a huge variety of symptoms associated with the condition. The most common one, apart from reading diffi-culties, is an inability to follow complex instructions. Dyslexia is associated with a rather poor working memory and sets of complex instructions simply get forgotten halfway through. Dyslexics also tend to have difficulty with time and frequently cannot sense how much time has passed. This is often shown when asking a child to be ready in ten minutes and the child hasn't even started getting ready when the time is over. Frequently, there is also a confusion between left and right.

Another typical symptom is that dyslexic youngsters often need longer to gather their thoughts than others. This can cause them great embarrassment at school when called upon to answer a question. Most teachers will want an immediate answer and will frown if it isn't forthcoming. (This is changing as teachers are becoming more aware of the issues.) Dyslexics also sometimes confuse words that they don't have to use often and will choose another word from a similar idea group. The standard example is that they may say volcano when they mean tornado or vice versa.

You can see that these symptoms can cause problems in school if they are not recognized as being dyslexia. They can easily be seen as a lack of cooperation and attention. This is inevitably going to lead to conflict with teachers. This, in turn, can lead to bad behaviour. If a youngster in class isn't getting down to the work and completing it on time, there are only two options open to him. He can either be sitting doing nothing or he can be making trouble. Neither of those are likely to lead to either an effective education or to a happy school-life.

Schools are making huge strides in helping dyslexic children reach their potential. They are becoming more and more aware of the special gifts of these youngsters and are catering more to their strengths and focusing less on their weaknesses. Many teachers will now accept a mind map as a homework from a dyslexic youngster rather than a piece of extended writing.

That, of course, is only true for those youngsters who are recognized as being dyslexic. There is probably a large number who have not been diagnosed and who are simply seen as being problem children. If you think that your teenager is one of these, an interview with someone at the school is urgently needed and a proper assessment made. The help is only available to those students who are properly identified.

If your teenager is dyslexic, there are many things that you can do to help him. They are all based on those three things that we parents have in profusion and sometimes keep hidden. They are simply these: love, compassion and respect. The one thing that absolutely must be avoided is ridicule. Remember: you don't help people do good by making them feel bad.

Your dyslexic teenager may be having a hard time of it at school with the work and possibly with unfeeling school-mates. You can help him get over these indignities with sensible love and affirmations. Let him know that you love and respect him and that other people being nasty isn't his problem – it's their problem. You don't want or need to protect him from the world. You need to give him the armour to go out into the world and allow the arrows of nastiness to bounce off harmlessly.

I have today discovered a technique that is helping my dyslexic son. He was transferring numbers to and from a calculator and doing it one digit at a time. I taught him how to group three or four digits together, put them into short-term memory and enter them straight away. The first five problems took him eight minutes. Then I taught him the technique. The remaining five problems took two minutes.

These practical little steps are easy to find when you look for them and they can make an enormous difference. My son was so happy. What a wonderful investment of five minutes of my time and his. I advise you to look for all opportunities to do the same.

Dysphasia

The common term for dysphasia is Specific Language Impairment (SLI) which describes it pretty well. When a child of normal or better intelligence has language abilities that are significantly lower than non-language abilities it is described as dysphasia. It is more common for youngsters to have difficulties in understanding (reception) than in explaining themselves (production).

This dysfunction often appears to reduce as the child grows and becomes a teenager, but it never completely disappears. It appears that the affected youngsters learn to avoid difficult situations where they need to understand complex language. It is difficult for them to improve their skills.

Dysphasia can also cause difficulties in reading. We need to be careful here to distinguish reading difficulties and normal or even advanced language skills consistent with dyslexia and reading difficulties caused by language difficulties consistent with dysphasia. The two are significantly different. The causes are different and the remedies are different.

It is possibly an inherited feature, but this is by no means well proven. There is certainly no single identified gene for the condition and it is more likely to be a complex combination of genes. As with dyslexia, there is some difficulty holding things in working memory and some of the same information channels in the brain are impaired. When you read or hear a sentence, you don't understand the full meaning until it is finished. When this memory doesn't work well, the beginning is forgotten before the end is reached. This problem makes learning anything difficult. Even highly educated adults have difficulty with sentences of eighteen words or more.

Dysphasic youngsters are frequently inattentive to language. As one researcher put it, 'They just don't seem to have their language antennas out all the time, only when they concentrate on language.' They will frequently not even pay attention to their own names being called. They have limited ability to understand subtle and abstract language which makes learning some subjects next to impossible.

This inattention and poor ability to follow instructions is frequently misunderstood as naughtiness, lack of concentration or lack of cooperation. This can lead to conflict and poor relations with teachers and school. Dysphasics have to get a different type of education. They simply will never thrive in a situation where language skills are demanded. They have to be able to learn through seeing and doing. Mind Mapping, videos and films, pictures, graphs and charts and so on are fine, but the written and spoken word are unlikely to ever get through.

If you suspect that your teenager is dysphasic and he is not getting the type of education he needs, you really do need to have this checked out. The school will be able to arrange this for you. As with dyslexia, you would expect the school to provide an education that is rich in pictures and activity rather than books and lectures for dysphasic youngsters.

If your teenager is dysphasic, there are certain things that you can do at home that the school probably can't do easily or as well. The most important of these is to teach him to look as well as listen. Communication experts agree that most information is carried by visual information. Your teenager will miss out on this, and probably on the listening as well, if he doesn't look at the speaker. If he doesn't answer when you call his name, a gentle touch on the shoulder to attract his attention is needed. Then make sure that you have good eye contact and give positive messages, not negative ones.

Dyscalculia

Although about half of the world doesn't get along with maths, dyscalculia is something much more profound and rare. It is thought to affect less than one per cent of the population but some estimates put it at as high as six per cent. It is a little-known and under-studied dysfunction. Many maths teachers have never even heard of it.

There are two types of dyscalculia that have been identified. Both of them refer to people with normal or better intelligence. They are called Primary and Secondary Dyscalculia. They refer to a disability with numbers and an inability to understand shape.

Primary Dyscalculia is connected with problems with working memory and is thought to be due to one or more areas of the brain being deficient. People with dyscalculia find it difficult to add up even small numbers beyond about ten.

Ideas of subtraction, multiplication and division become almost impossible. A feature appears to be that primary dyscalculics sometimes suddenly catch on to ideas in higher mathematics even though they retain problems with arithmetic. Albert Einstein was an example of this. It is reported that he kept multiplication tables on the walls of his office to help him. He once told a group of students that no matter what difficulty they had with maths, his difficulty was greater.

Secondary Dyscalculia is associated with shape and space as well as number. Youngsters with this problem find maths much more difficult as they advance through the school system. Ideas of geometry and equations and the like are impossible to comprehend. In extreme cases, they can even become lost on their way to and from well-known places. Youngsters with this dysfunction generally cannot read maps, so this may be a useful diagnostic tool.

Dyscalculia is often only a part of a host of dysfunctions. For this reason, it is often not picked up at school. The teenager is seen as being of low ability generally (even though this is probably not true), so the lack of progress in maths is only to be expected.

If you suspect that your teenager is dyscalculic, you must contact the school and have the situation investigated. It is unlikely to be picked up and acted upon otherwise. There are limited things that schools can do to help overcome the difficulties, but at least your teenager can be spared the pain of being thought stupid when this is not the case.

Dyspraxia

The 'praxia' part of the name for this condition comes from the word praxis which (in this sense) means the practical ability to live efficiently and effectively. The old-fashioned name for this dysfunction is 'Clumsy Child Syndrome', and it describes it fairly well. But there is more to it than that. Dyspraxia is also an emotional immaturity. It is thought to affect maybe one in twenty youngsters with average or better intelligence, with four out of five of them being boys. It isn't usually diagnosed until secondary school. Many younger children aren't well coordinated so the dysfunction can remain hidden in a sea of similarly clumsy children! Dyspraxics often develop strategies to fit in with their friends.

Also, the level of personal organization needed at secondary school is much higher and dyspraxics find this difficult.

There is no certain cause of dyspraxia, but it is thought to be due to brain cells not maturing at the normal rate. This means that the brain takes longer to process information and makes it more likely that information will get lost. It hasn't been linked to brain damage or any specific area of the brain, so it's all a bit of a mystery really.

The symptoms, however, aren't much of a mystery. Maybe the most obvious is significant emotional immaturity. He probably has very few friends except for maybe a similar child. He causes excessive disruption in class, has lots of temper tantrums at home and nearly always has poor posture and physical coordination.

If your teenager is dyspraxic, the school will almost certainly know about it and have let you know. Dyspraxic youngsters frequently can and do cause problems for themselves and everyone else in their class. If you suspect that your teenager is dyspraxic and the school isn't aware, then you need to get this looked into as soon as possible. Dyspraxia is often linked to late development of milestones in younger childhood such as walking and first words. If your teenager is investigated this will certainly be looked into.

There are no cures for dyspraxia, but it can be greatly helped by effective teaching in special groups or maybe one-on-one. A dyspraxic teenager can learn the necessary social skills and practical skills given sufficient help and guidance from a sympathetic and skilled teacher. Nearly every school will have a special teacher with the qualifications and experience to help. These expert and dedicated individuals can work wonders given sufficient time and rapport with teenagers.

At home, you really do need to help your teenager develop life strategies. Here's a nice example: one lady I heard of has recorded a tape of pleasant relaxing music and put her own voice onto it between tracks. She starts playing the tape at 7.30 sharp every morning. At the end of each track there is something like, 'Luke, it's time to finish breakfast now and go brush your teeth.' Then some time later, 'It's time to put your school bag by the door now, Luke.' There is no chasing up to be done and the teenager knows that, so he is developing the maturity to go with it. Mum gets to keep her temper and not have to be on Luke's case every minute of every morning. This is brilliant!

Other strategies involve checklists of things to be done before bed or maybe checking in with Mum or Dad at regular intervals to show that tasks have been completed and life is progressing normally. You can be as creative as you like with this one. Just help your teenager to get through life with as few problems as possible and develop simple systems.

You should also encourage lots of outdoor activity like walking and cycling in the park, if possible. Although the dyspraxic brain will never become fully mature, any form of physical exercise coupled with a good diet will help it get into better condition. Also, a body with well-toned muscles is going to have better posture than the alternative.

Autism and Asperger's Syndrome

The single word autism covers a range of conditions with a range of severities and with a number of different causes. If a child is severely autistic, the diagnosis would have been made quite early in life, at about age three or even less. At the other end of this broad spectrum, it may not be diagnosed until secondary school. This is often the case with Asperger's Syndrome which is usually thought of as being a mild form of autism. (There are some experts who disagree with this, however, and consider it to be a separate condition.)

The modern understanding of autism is mainly due to the work of Lorna Wing and Judith Gould, who worked in London in the late 1970s. Autism is now understood to be a grouping of three impairments: social impairment, language impairment and repetitive behaviour. Autism is only diagnosed if these three are found together.

Both children and adults with autism sometimes behave as if other people simply do not exist. They don't respond to cuddles and hugs and are often expressionless except for extremes of joy or anger. They often appear to be living most of their lives in a little world all of their own. People with Asperger's Syndrome, on the other hand, frequently want to make friends, but find it difficult. Common speech problems are things like missing out all but the most important words. Something like "go car shop" is quite enough information. They can also have a very literal understanding of language and not understand ideas such as the metaphor 'raining cats and dogs'. They like routine and order in their lives and any upset can cause extreme reactions. Their lack of social awareness leads to a real difficulty in making friends and can cause a whole host of inappropriate (to you and me) behaviours. Occasionally, autistic people can have incredible mental abilities in certain areas like mathematics. The movie *Rain Man* was about one such (fictitious) person.

If you have any concerns that your teenager may be autistic or have Asperger's Syndrome, a trip to the doctor is needed. The diagnosis of these conditions really does need to be made by an expert, so the doctor will refer you to specialists. You ought also inform the school of your suspicions and keep in close contact with them.

The Rule of Three

If your teenager has difficulty following instructions, you can borrow an idea from the US Marine Corps. The rule is that no set of instructions should contain more than three things. Each one instruction should be clear and easily remembered. An example at home might be something like, 'John, would you please get your shower now, put your dirty clothes in the wash box and get into your bedclothes.' It may be a good idea to ask your teenager to repeat them back to you to make sure that they have registered. The Marines found that three instructions was the ideal number to get the job done correctly. If four were given at one time, performance dropped hugely. I predict you will find the same.

Make sure that you have clear and simple systems for your teenager to follow. Every morning and evening should follow a similar routine with the same things happening at the same time. Here's a piece of advice: don't try to re-create the people in your house to suit your systems. If there are any difficulties, re-agree the systems (Win-Win, remember) and make sure that they suit the people in your house. This is the simplest way of avoiding conflict and getting to a consistent agreement.

Parent Partnership Services

Youngsters with learning difficulties frequently have quite difficult behaviour as well, and this can be wearing and upsetting for parents. Local Education Authorities (LEAs) have a legal obligation to provide information, advice and support for parents of SEN youngsters via Parent Partnership Services (PPS). They 'work to bring together schools, parents and others to promote positive outcomes for children with Special Educational Needs'.

If you feel that you need any kind of help and support – and this can be anything from a sympathetic ear to advice on legal matters – get in contact with your teenager's school and ask for the phone number of the PPS or go direct to the LEA.

Review

- A small number of youngsters of average intelligence or better may be affected by learning disorders. The reasons for these are not well understood and there are no cures, as such. All of them can be improved by specialist teaching and a sympathetic and effective approach at home.
- Some youngsters may require specialist help at some time in their school career. Schools are aware of this and provide all the help they can.
- If you feel that you need help, contact the Parent Partnership Service provided by your Local Education Authority.

Action Exercises

■ If your teenager has difficulty in getting the job done, learn and use the US Marines' Rule of Three. Always give sets of three easily understood and followed instructions.

■ Create simple systems for living. Remember to make systems for people and don't try to re-create the people to suit your systems.

■ Make the time to play games at home. Scrabble and other word games can really help dyslexic children with word recognition and spelling. Card games, Yahtzee and other number games are ideal for number work. Juggling is excellent for balancing the two hemispheres of the brain and improving hand-eye coordination. Memory games like Kim's Game or Queen's Carpet can be helpful to train the short-term memory.

TWELVE

Nurturing Your Teenager

Start with the end in mind

Somehow, the idea of nurturing a teenager sometimes seems a bit odd. They want and need lots of independence and give all the appearance of wanting as little help as possible. This is a false impression. There is plenty of research that shows that teenagers want and very much need parental love, guidance and real physical and moral care. They will rarely admit to it, but they know that they need the limits and guidance that we have to offer.

We are parents. We can't help but love our teenagers. Even when they appear to be unlovable and infuriating, we love them still. We have an inalienable right and duty to show them that love in every way that we can. The way that we nurture them day in and day out is a real and practical demonstration of that love.

Family time

Your teenager needs time for friends, fun and family. The better the time he spends with family, the better he will enjoy it and come to value it. It's your job to adapt family time to the teenager in your house. You can't expect him to adapt himself to you. He is changing and growing, and the things that he'll want to do are changing and growing as well.

Family meals are always much more pleasant when everybody is together at the table. It's a lovely way to have family time. You can make any mealtime a little bit special by turning down the lights and lighting a candle and maybe having a bottle of plonk or cider to go with the food. You can make a mealtime extra special if you make it a celebration meal. Why not celebrate any achievement that your teenager makes? How about sending out for an extra special pizza when your teenager brings home a merit certificate or reports an improving grade in a class? Life offers many opportunities for celebrations besides just birthdays and anniversaries.

Another way of making family time a little bit special is to have regular or irregular one-on-one 'Family Dates' with each other. Maybe Mother and Son can go out together once a week or a fortnight to somewhere a little bit special and have real one-on-one time. It may be just a regular shopping trip, but you make it extra special by stopping off at Macdonalds or having an espresso on the way back. Maybe Dad could take daughter to the cinema or even for a nice walk in the park. It's not only toddlers and grannies that feed the ducks, you know. You can easily think up things to do that will give you private and real quality time together.

I have to go to an office supplies store regularly and usually take one of my boys with me. They can go and get some of the things I need while I lust after some new shiny gadget. When the shopping is over, we walk round together and discuss what things might be good for the business and what we could live quite happily without. I make sure that the conversation in the car there and back is always very him-centred. I find out all about what happens at school, about their thoughts, likes, dislikes and concerns. I hear them growing up in the things they say and the profound questions they sometimes ask. Simple and powerful stuff.

We also have a family video night every Friday. My wife takes the kids down to the library and they take it in turns to choose a video. Then they come back and we have homemade Daddyburgers and something a little special to drink. There are often assorted friends draped over chairs and the floor and sometimes aunts, uncles and cousins come round and share this time with us as well. It's not much more than a little family ritual, but it's a part of the way we think of ourselves.

These are simple and cheap things to do. It's never the complexity or expense factor that's important. It's the mere fact that we spend good, quality time getting to know each other ever more deeply and sharing our love in a practical way. Get into the habit of looking for things that will enhance your family life and the quality of your time together.

Nutrition

Teenagers know this even better than you and I, but they still try as hard as possible to deny it. Good nutrition is vital for good health. Teenage bodies are still growing, as are their brains. They must be supplied with the right amounts of the right foods in the right balance. A diet of pizza, burgers, crisps, sweet bars and fizzy drinks is not going to build up a healthy body. We need a good, healthy balance of the different food groups in the right amount. We also need plenty of fresh fruit and vegetables to get the vitamins and trace minerals essential for good health.

It is estimated that westerners consume several kilograms of artificial and quite unnecessary chemicals every year in doses of a few milligrams here and a few more there. Many of these chemicals are known to have serious negative effects on the behaviour of some children. There are many schools now which are refusing to serve foods or sell sweets containing these chemicals. A few schools have encouraged parents to experiment with eliminating them from their children's diet. All schools all over the UK and in the US that have done this have reported noticeable improvements in children's performance and behaviour.

There is significant scientific evidence to support the idea that good nutrition improves behaviour. Experiments conducted at prisons in the US and in the UK have shown that many people show greatly improved behaviour when vitamin and other dietary deficiencies are remedied. Other scientific studies in US schools have shown that diets that eliminate refined foods and drinks can improve behaviour and academic performance significantly.

The brain as well as the body needs adequate nutrition. The brain is an electro-chemical device that uses many hundreds of different chemicals to operate. If nutrition doesn't supply them, then brain function will either be impaired or, at the least, slowed down. The brain needs a chemical called omega-3 fatty acid to provide the insulation on brain cells and other cells in the nervous system. This is only found in oily fish – notoriously absent in the teenage diet – and some nuts. (Your granny was right. Fish IS brain food.) The brain also needs a variety of proteins and vitamins to create the neurotransmitters that allow it to work properly and quickly. If they are absent, the brain won't function as well as it should. You might want to consider vitamin supplements or supplemental fish oils containing omega-3 fatty acids.

I have to admit that none of this scientific research is without its critics. Most of the criticism is from the food industry, but also some is from independent respected medical sources. In spite of this, I believe that the message is quite clear. There is no research which shows that a good, healthy, balanced diet is bad for you. There is research that shows that an inadequate diet is bad for you. I would prefer to err on the side of caution and go for non-processed, fresh foods whenever possible. I would advise you to do the same.

I know of one parent of a teenager who seems to agree with me quite independently. She was concerned about her son's behaviour at school and at home. Luckily, the boy himself recognized that something was wrong as well. They discussed the possibilities and agreed to try a change of diet away from processed foods and towards a balanced diet of unprocessed foods. The difference was wonderful to behold. He is now a happy and well-adjusted young man and doing extremely well at school whereas before he was exactly the opposite. The difference took only a week to show itself.

There is plenty of information available about what a good diet is and isn't. Your teenager gets plenty of PSHE at school, so is probably even more aware of it than you are. Talk about this seriously together and design your own family regime. As an added bonus, you will find that eating healthily can actually cost a lot less than buying over-priced and over-packaged de-natured foods.

Sleep

You knock on your older teenager's door in the morning. What do you hear? 'Yes, Mum. I'm getting up now.' No, you certainly don't. If you're lucky, you'll get a grunt. When he eventually does get up, he's like a bear with a sore paw and staggers around bleary-eyed and grumpy. Conversation at breakfast, if he gets there at all, is limited to say the least. Yes, you've got a standard issue teenager who simply doesn't get enough sleep.

This is another one that teenagers will deny as loudly and as long as they possibly can, but it's nonetheless true for that. Teenagers need at least nine hours sleep a night. If they don't get it, they reduce their ability to learn and think. Tests done at universities and sleep research centres the world over have come up with findings that won't surprise anyone.

Sleep is essential for learning. The brain actually processes the day's learning experiences, both of things learned in school and in life in general. If there isn't enough sleep, the brain doesn't process the learning properly and the learning doesn't get done anything like effectively. Also, if students are sleepy in lessons, they aren't in a good mental state to learn. The brainwave frequencies are just too low. The fad for sleep learning that existed about twenty or so years ago has been found to be quite baseless.

One of the problems facing teenagers is that their body clocks seem to prevent them from feeling tired in the later part of the evening. They don't want to go to bed until they feel tired, which doesn't normally start until about ten o'clock. There is only one sensible solution to this problem. Teenagers need to be trained to get enough sleep.

The important thing is that they should have a regular regime for going to bed. This should be something such as: no TV after about half past nine, listening to relaxing music and reading for twenty minutes or so, a relaxing bath or shower and then in bed by ten o'clock in a dark room. Any later than this and they are going to be deprived of sleep and learn less well. They are also going to be miserable and grumpy for most of the early part of the next day.

This system works because of the brainwaves discussed in Chapter 11. It seems that brainwave frequency can accelerate very fast, but only slows down over quite a long period of time. That means that it is difficult to get a good night's sleep if teenagers go to bed immediately after watching an exciting movie on TV or playing video games. For the brainwaves to slow down sufficiently for sleep to come quickly, relaxation must be gradual and extended over twenty to thirty minutes.

Review

- Even teenagers need nurturing. You can provide this by making sure that your family changes and grows with the teenager and provides for changing needs. Quality family time is just as important as ever.
- Teenagers' nutritional needs are best met by an adequate diet. Many authorities suggest that inadequate nutrition and artificial chemicals in food have a negative effect on teenagers' behaviour and intelligence. The scientific evidence is disputed, but it is better to err on the side of caution.
- There is no doubt that a lack of sleep causes many attention and learning problems as well as behaviour problems in teenagers. Teenagers need to be trained how to get good quality sleep.

Action Exercises

- Design family life to suit the changing needs of your teenager and others.

- Make special family times throughout the week. Invite friends and other family to join you sometimes.

- Have one-on-one time with every family member.

- Discuss diet and nutrition with your teenager. Go for a healthy balance of unprocessed foods and drinks whenever possible.

- Design a regular bedtime routine that will help your teenager go to sleep quickly and get enough sleep.

Further Reading

My opinion is that, apart from this book, these two additional books are all that you could ever need in the quest to create a happy and fulfilling family life and bring up happy, healthy teenagers. They are both variations on the groundbreaking 7 Habits theme created by Dr Stephen Covey. I recommend both books highly.

Covey, Stephen, *The 7 Habits of Highly Effective Families*, New York: Simon & Schuster, 1998

Covey, Sean, *The 7 Habits of Highly Effective Teens*, New York: Simon & Schuster, 1999

Index